MW00627862

CAN'T LIVE WITH 'EM, CAN'T LIVE WITHOUT 'EM

STEPHEN F. ARTERBURN, MEd

DAVID A. STOOP, PhD

W PUBLISHING GROUP
A Division of Thomas Nelson Publishers
Since 1798
www.wpublishinggroup.com

CAN'T LIVE WITH 'EM, CAN'T LIVE WITHOUT 'EM

Copyright © 1988 by Stephen F. Arterburn and David A. Stoop

Previously published under the title *When Someone You Love Is Someone You Hate*

All rights reserved. No portion of this book may be reproduced, stored in a retrieval system, or transmitted in any form or by any means—electronic, mechanical, photocopy, recording, or any other—except for brief quotations in printed reviews, without the prior written permission of the publisher.

Published by W Publishing Group, a Division of Thomas Nelson, Inc., P.O. Box 141000, Nashville, Tennessee 37214.

W Publishing Group books may be purchased in bulk for educational, business, fund-raising, or sales promotional use. For information, please e-mail SpecialMarkets@ThomasNelson.com.

All Scripture quotations, unless otherwise indicated, are from The Holy Bible, New International Version. Copyright © 1973, 1978, 1984, International Bible Society. Used by permission of Zondervan.

Library of Congress Cataloging-in-Publication Data

Arterburn, Stephen, 1953–
    [When someone you love is someone you hate]
    Can't live with 'em, can't live without 'em / Stephen F. Arterburn & David A. Stoop.
        p. cm.
    Originally published: When someone you love is someone you hate. Word, c1988.
    Includes bibliographical references and index.
    1. Love-hate relationships—Religious aspects—Christianity. I. Stoop, David A. II. Title.
    BV4597.53.C58A78 2006
    158.2—dc22   2006008878

Printed in the United States of America
06 07 08 09 10 RRD 9 8 7 6 5 4 3 2 1

This work is dedicated to our wonderful parents.
They taught us to love unconditionally, without
expectation.
More important, however, they taught us how to
forgive and to forgive again.

Contents

———— ∞ ————

Chapter One

LOVING THE ONE YOU HATE; HATING THE ONE YOU LOVE

ALMOST EVERYONE HAS AT LEAST ONE—A PERSON YOU deeply love and care about while at the same time you deeply resent and hate. The June 9, 1988, Issue of *USA Today* featured a cover story with the headline, "He Loves Her, He Loves Her Not." It is a story about the marriage of James Brown, the "Godfather of Soul." The article states that "he'd stomped on her foot so hard it left a boot mark. He's hit her, bruising her badly enough to send her to University Hospital. When she tried to escape, he'd grabbed a pistol and shot at their white Lincoln." That's what his wife told the police. But they still live together.

When he was interviewed, Brown said, "'I love her. She's my sugar-wuger.' The next minute, he says he's going ahead with a divorce." When his wife was interviewed later, she said, "We're fine. We're not going to get a divorce. We are still one soul. We are still in love."

Most love-hate relationships don't make the newspaper.

They are more insidious than that. They don't seem that dramatic most of the time; but the end result is the same—love and hate.

SARAH: BUCKS, BOOZE, AND A BROKEN HEART

For Sarah, her love-hate relationship was with her father. Dad had always been able to make a lot of money, and his love for that money was surpassed only by his love for alcohol. As an adult child of an alcoholic, Sarah has struggled with the expression of her own emotions for a long time. She feels totally confused within. So she has tried to learn not to feel emotions at all. The more her dad continues to drink, the more Sarah can't stand to be around him. But she can't stay away from him either. At the core of her dilemma is a father who will not provide Sarah with what she wants most—the emotional closeness that has been denied her.

Growing up, Sarah's family life was like walking on eggshells. Mother was there, but she was preoccupied with Dad, trying to keep his drinking under control. Any problems that arose could usually be solved with money. As a result, Sarah got everything she wanted materially. And when, as an adolescent, she created trouble, money put out the fire.

It was during this time that Sarah starting looking for emotional closeness elsewhere. Most of the guys she went out with were older, and it didn't take long for her to end up in their bedrooms. But these relationships didn't last very long, for as soon as Sarah did begin to get close to someone, she would just as quickly walk away.

Sarah is only twenty-six, but she feels as though she has lived a lot more years than that. Several times, the feelings of isolation have become so intense that she has made a serious attempt at suicide; but those attempts only led to big emotional battles with her dad in the hospital. After feeling his anger and rejection, she'd grit her teeth and swear she would never see her dad again, only to find herself several weeks later bringing a new boyfriend over to meet her parents.

Sarah's friends can see the torture she is putting herself through, but they have given up trying to make her see the pattern. Sarah is blind to the dynamic of what she is doing. She's caught in the double bind of loving and searching for something she cannot have—at least not from the person she insists on having it from. She hates the one she loves and idolizes.

All of her relationships suffer. She limits herself, partly out of the fear that she will be rejected and hurt by others, and partly out of the feeling that she is not really good enough for anyone to *really* care about her. Sarah knows a lot of people; but down inside she is convinced that everyone knows what a worthless person she is. When others compliment her on anything, she is quick to point out her flaws. As a result, she feels so misunderstood and unacceptable that no one is able to make her feel okay—no one, that is, except Dad. And he won't.

People like Sarah often feel they are so needy inside that it is impossible for all of these needs ever to be satisfied. This leads them into a vicious cycle of depreciating love and caring from others because "it's just not enough." Almost every relationship Sarah has been in has eventually felt empty; it "wasn't enough."

One doesn't have to have an alcoholic parent to feel like

Sarah. Children who are raised in abusive family situations often find themselves in the same trap of seeking love and approval from a hated parent. To those not raised in that kind of family environment, it seems incredulous that anyone would seek love and approval from an abusive parent; but we do. It seems that the less love we experience, the more we seek it from the person who can't—or won't—give it.

MARY: ABANDONED IN RAGE

Mary, a friend of Sarah, understands what Sarah is struggling with. She has many of the same feelings. While Mary's mother was pregnant with her, her father left; he literally abandoned both his wife and daughter. It wasn't until Mary was an adult that she was able to look for her dad. Her mother had remarried, and Mary was fortunate to have had a wonderful stepfather. But there was still a hole inside Mary that only her real dad could fill. She was filled with rage at this unknown father for abandoning her; but she also longed deeply for his love and approval. And while she both hated and loved her absent father, Mary also searched for assurance that her mother's devotion to her was genuine.

Sometimes a parent can be too caring for the child, and the loving attention can seem fake. The overprotective or the overcontrolling parent often leaves the child with a hollow feeling that the caring parent is not really that caring. Help or gifts that come even before they are needed begin to feel automatic, like the response of a robot. We wonder what the parent *really* feels down inside. Are they doing this because they have to? Do they really care? It's almost too good to be true, so we end up not trusting it. Then we set about searching for affirmation that the parent really does care about us and love us—a task that sets off the same vicious cycle Sarah experienced with her alcoholic father.

In each situation, the person is trapped in a cycle that alternates between loving the parent and hating the parent. Mixed in is a lot of guilt for being unable to resolve the dilemma. Sarah and Mary had decisions to make.

JOE AND BETTY: PERPLEXED PARENTS

Sometimes the problem goes in the opposite direction. Joe and Betty feel like giving up. Their fifteen-year-old son has embarrassed and disgraced them so many times they have lost count. He wears some of the strangest clothes—they look like they were used in a horror movie. All of his friends—that is, the few he has left—dress just as he does. Their hair changes color weekly and usually sticks straight up in greased-together spikes.

Until recently, Joe and Betty had tried to accept Daren's behavior, thinking it would pass. They insisted that he eat with them in restaurants and come with them to family outings. But his obnoxious and rude behavior had become more than they could tolerate. The last time they took him to a restaurant, his behavior was so awful they left without eating.

Whenever they tried to talk with Daren, they usually ended up in an angry confrontation, with Daren screaming that he wished they were dead. The last confrontation had actually frightened both Joe and Betty; they came seeking counseling.

At their first session, which Daren refused to attend, it was obvious that the parents wanted a quick fix for this out-of-control problem. But when they came to understand there was no easy answer to their dilemma, they kept coming to therapy—for themselves.

As they explored their own feelings about their son, they became aware of their own frightening wish that Daren was dead. They were overwhelmed with guilt over these feelings. And of course Daren took advantage of their confusion to pit his parents against each other and ultimately get what he wanted. In these situations, one parent became overwhelmed by anger and even hatred, while the other parent was overwhelmed by guilt mixed with love. In one confrontation one parent would be angry; in the next confrontation the other parent would take the angry-parent role. Joe and Betty alternated in and out of their love-hate/guilt-anger roles.

As is so often true in a love-hate relationship, one person uses the mixed feelings to manipulate and get what he or she wants from the other. In this situation, Daren never needed to look at himself. He could blame everything on his parents and the messed-up system.

Joe and Betty realized that the harder they tried to fix Daren, the worse his behavior became. Because they didn't know what else to do, and didn't seem to have the power to change Daren, they ended up feeling helpless.

Joe and Betty are experiencing a confusion between helplessness and powerlessness. There is an important difference. In the course of therapy, Joe and Betty learned they are truly *powerless* in their efforts to change or control Daren's behavior. But they are not *helpless*. There are some important steps they can take, and they had already taken one of them—they sought help from someone trained to give it.

They can also change their expectations for Daren and limit the public contact they have with him. They can learn to ignore some behaviors while consistently and together confronting other more important issues with Daren. Joe and Betty may be powerless; but they are not helpless in their love-hate dilemma. There is a decision for them to make.

DAN: TROUBLED EMPLOYEE

Dan faces a different dilemma. His love-hate relationship is at work. Dan started with his company right out of college. Within five years he was a senior vice president with the firm. His rapid success was largely due to his boss, who was moving up ahead of him in the company. He opened all the doors for Dan.

It sounds like the ideal situation—except that Dan's boss was a power monger. He wasn't satisfied with his success; he wanted more. As a result, he couldn't share any accomplishments with Dan or anyone else. The boss even expected Dan to give him credit for the things Dan really did on his own.

The boss held Dan's success over his head. He frequently reminded him of why he had been so quickly promoted. Dan really appreciated everything his boss had done to help him, but he also felt a growing resentment toward his boss. These feelings grew within him to the point that he actually began to dread going to work. When he was at the office, he avoided his boss as much as possible. He felt trapped. He couldn't leave; but more and more he felt that he couldn't stay either. Dan came for help when he had a series of dreams, each one ending with his killing his boss in a different way.

As Dan began to explore his relationship with his boss, he started to see that his self-confidence had been gradually eroded by the boss's behavior. He had been brainwashed into believing that if he left the company, he would be a failure, since all of his success was due only to his boss. He was paralyzed by his loyalty to his boss and the feelings of dependency that had developed.

Dan knew that his boss had helped him get ahead; but he also knew that he was good at what he did and his aptitude had played a significant part in his success. He felt trapped. On the one hand, he had a deep respect for his boss. But on the other hand, he deeply resented him for the way he expected Dan to behave. His loss of self-confidence had made it difficult for him to see any other alternative to his predicament. He had a decision to make.

SANDRA: SLEEPING WITH THE PAST

Sandra is a thirty-two-year-old mother of two boys, ages six and eight. She is a single parent. Her divorce was final two years ago, but it has been five years since Ray, her ex-husband, left to pursue a career in music. Ray is a classic example of the irresponsible husband who left his family to pursue his own dream. The years that Sandra and Ray were married were rocky and unstable times. Ray had left several times before, once with another woman. Over the years, Sandra had grown to hate him; but she never would have left or challenged the relationship.

When Ray made it clear the last time that he wasn't coming back, Sandra was relieved—and saddened, too. She hated his impulsiveness and irresponsibility, but she enjoyed his companionship. Now that he's really gone, she misses having Ray around and feels depressed and lonely. She's concerned now that Ray stays involved with the boys. "They need a father," she keeps reminding herself.

Although she is determined not to do it, each time he comes to see the boys (which isn't very often), he persuades her to let him stay the night and sleep with her. Every time, she awakes the next morning with a feeling of disgust. She struggles with her feelings of loneliness and her fear that if she doesn't give in, he will stop coming to see the boys. As she talks about Ray, there is still a spark of feeling as she remembers the good times of the past.

Sandra is caught on a treadmill of values that bounce between her hurt and anger at Ray's irresponsibility and rejection of her, her own needs and loneliness, and the intense fear that if she stands up for herself, the boys will lose their father. The more she struggles with her dilemma, the more she hates Ray for putting her in such an awful place.

Sandra knows that she needs to extend her life beyond Ray in order to feel good about herself; but every time he comes over, he begins to talk about the good times and she ends up giving in to his request to stay over. Sandra begins to feel that she is a victim: helpless, unable to do anything to change her situation. When she stops and thinks about it, she realizes she still has feelings of love for Ray, but she is so frustrated by the way things are, she feels resentment and hatred for him, too.

It's hard for a victim to make a decision, but Sandra needs to make one.

MARILYN: OH GOD!

Marilyn lived in a small town where everyone knew everyone else, and also knew everything about everyone else. She and her husband, Tom, had been married for eighteen years. Tom's job took him out of town often, and eventually it took him into a relationship with another woman. Marilyn and Tom struggled together in secret for over a year; but finally, Tom filed for divorce. As soon as the court record hit the newspaper, rumors started flying fast and furiously, and Marilyn was the focus of all of the town's gossip.

As is often the case, some people were downright cruel. Several stopped her at the store and asked her what she had done to drive "poor Tom" away. She was hurt, humiliated, and angry. She didn't want the divorce, but she was beginning to hate Tom for the problems he was creating for her.

About halfway through the divorce process, Tom suffered severe chest pains. Before the paramedics arrived, he had a cardiac arrest, and despite efforts to revive him, he was pronounced dead when they arrived at the hospital. Marilyn's anger went from her husband directly to God. How could God have allowed such a thing? How could He allow her to suffer the public humiliation of the affair and the divorce if Tom was going to die anyway? All she could think was one big WHY?

Now, two years later, Marilyn has not been inside a church since Tom died. In fact, she seldom leaves her home. She's still too humiliated to face any of the people in the town. Her love-hate relationship is with God, and right now it is mostly hate. She doesn't know how she feels about Tom. He was just a victim in God's strange, twisted plan—at least that's how she sees it.

Her love-hate relationship with God has infected all of her relationships. She finally came for help after an explosive confrontation with her daughter. She told the counselor that her daughter had given up on her and now she was left with absolutely no one. Tom had died on her. And God had betrayed her. And now her daughter didn't understand her.

Marilyn's situation was complex because the unexpected death of her husband didn't allow her to work out her feelings of anger and hurt toward him. When he died, all of these negative feelings were projected onto God. Also, since Marilyn did not want the divorce, the early death of her husband did not allow her to work out the possibility of reconciliation. Marilyn believed God messed up the situation by letting Tom die before anything could be worked out. At this point, Marilyn did not know whether her anger and hatred were focused on Tom or on God.

Her problem was complicated by the fact that all of us tend to idealize those who have died. It's hard to really feel anger or hatred toward someone who is dead, even if those feelings are justified. In her avoidance of dealing with Tom's death, all of Marilyn's confused feelings were focused on God. Her love-hate relationship with Tom became a love-hate relationship with God. She had some important decisions to make to begin to sort out this one.

LOVING AND HATING MYSELF

We've looked at five individuals who experienced a love-hate relationship in their lives. You may have noticed a common undercurrent in all of them: it didn't matter if the object of the love-hate relationship was a parent, a child, a boss, a mate, or God; the end result was that the feelings of love and hate were ultimately turned inward upon themselves. Each one—Sarah, Mary, Joe and Betty, Dan, Sandra, and Marilyn—ended up feeling a confused mixture of love and hatred toward themselves.

The result of this love-hate feeling being turned inward is lowered self-esteem. And when self-esteem is lowered, it sets off a destructive cycle that seems to have no end. As one gets caught in this destructive cycle, the positive solutions to the dilemma seem to disappear, and he or she feels even more trapped than before. The more one feels trapped, the more self-esteem is lowered—and on and on it goes.

When people are caught in this vicious cycle, feelings become so painful and overwhelming that the only way to survive seems to be to stop feeling at all. We attempt to stop only the painful, negative feelings, but that's not the way emotions work. What we do with one set of emotions is what we will do with all of our emotions. The end result is detachment from all emotions. We no longer know what it is we really do feel.

THE LOSS OF FEELINGS

People who are caught in a love-hate relationship can often detach themselves from their feelings. But they cannot be with the person they both love and hate very long. If they are, all of the hurt and hate start boiling up inside and they feel out of control. It's as if their emotions are frozen—in a deep freeze—except when they are with the person they both love and hate. Then the deep freeze begins to defrost, and the frozen feelings of hurt and pain begin to thaw out. And they can't bear that.

In each case the individual experiences tremendous internal turmoil. When someone or something reminds him or her of that painful relationship, his or her emotions contort into massive confusion and despair.

The problem is intensified because we feel so powerless. We are frustrated by our inability to fix things, and yet we're almost addicted to the process of trying.

Just as in the recovery process from an addiction, we must first distinguish between our feelings of powerlessness and helplessness. As long as we mistakenly believe that we can have some power over another person and his or her behavior, we will remain stuck in our misery of feeling powerless. What we are doing is part of what the Bible says is "a way that seems right to a man, but in the end it leads to death" (Prov. 14:12). We think we are on the right track, but the end is futile and empty, only giving us what we were trying to avoid.

To recover, we must accept our powerlessness but not our helplessness. We decide not to be helpless when we begin to look around for help. We cannot break our addiction to that love-hate relationship while living in isolation. We must reach out to someone else and ask for help.

And just as it was for each of the people we described in this chapter, the decision to ask for help is the first, and perhaps most important, decision you have to make. Your picking up this book and reading it may be your request for help. As you work through the issues in each chapter, you will be taking steps in the direction of recovery and wholeness. But first, let's look at why these love-hate relationships develop.

Chapter Two

WHY LOVE-HATE
RELATIONSHIPS DEVELOP

JAMES AND FAYE BLANCHARD WERE DEALING WITH THE worst nightmare imaginable for two parents in a small town in Georgia, or for parents anywhere. Their daughter, a talented twenty-six-year-old writer from New York, had come home to stay. Actually, she had come home to live out the rest of her life. With her she brought the virus that was killing thousands. Lisa Blanchard was dying of AIDS. Since her diagnosis the Blanchards had been nothing but supportive. They had opened their home to Lisa and pledged to meet her needs until the inevitable end came. They detested Lisa's lifestyle, but they were determined to show her their love when it was needed most. They were never negative around her, determined to spare her the sermons they had preached at her for years with no impact. It was their open display of love and acceptance that astounded Lisa and everyone else who knew of the Blanchards' dedication and sacrifice for their daughter.

Although their love poured out freely toward Lisa, between themselves it became thin and worn. James and Faye did not notice the initial signs of the strain in their partnership. It did not occur in one big resounding clash of anger. The cracks of discontent began to crumble their marriage into small fragments rather than large chunks. It began with a gradual diminishing of their usual laughter and humor. Their inside jokes were ignored. They did not play to the sense of parody they had learned to appreciate in each other.

So, slowly, they became bland and lifeless in their communication. The stagnation of their unity shrouded their togetherness like the death their daughter fought. Neither noticed as they became draped in this dull and remote atmosphere of depression.

As their daughter's illness dragged on, they needed each other's support all the more. But neither could give it to the other. Though they never said an angry word to their daughter, they began to criticize each other openly. They bit and snipped at the self-esteem that had already become fragile from the first moment of discovery of their daughter's fate. Neither could do right in the eyes of the other. A love and marriage that had been a motivating example to many became filled with bitterness, resentment, and anger.

After a year of learning to cope with Lisa's tragedy, neither could utter the words "I love you." Between the sound of those words and the desire to say them was a mass of rancor, hostility, and rage that choked off the expression that once characterized their affection. Now, like their daughter, their relationship was dying a bitter death. But unlike Lisa's life, their marriage could be saved. The threads of love and hate could be untangled, the cracks could be sealed, and the destruction of their union could be stopped.

Relationships that become destructive and saturated by bitterness, resentment, and hate do not result from accidental mysteries that are unsolvable. These combinations of sourced emotion do not "just happen." Love-hate relationships originate from an identifiable source, then progress along a predictable path, and are resolved with a proven prescription. Whether at the initiation or the final stages of the progressively more damaging relationship, the disastrous feelings surrounding each person can be resolved. Motivation for change and growth can occur. Hate can be removed and replaced with a mature foundation of nurturing and support that provides vibrancy and allows dynamic growth to overcome the stagnant relationship.

But before the problem can be fixed, it must be understood. In the case of love-hate relationships, the truth that leads to understanding is the source of freedom for the strugglers who are trapped and know no other resolution but separation or divorce. Searching for understanding is the first step in saving the relationship.

At the base of this confusing dichotomy of feeling, there are three negative emotions that combine to foster the development of the love-hate bind. These three emotions of great negative impact are fear, anger, and guilt. Within the dimensions of these powerful feelings lie the foundations for relationships that so many detest. The sources of fear, anger, and guilt must be identified, processed, and resolved in order for a relationship to become one of total love. The material that follows in this chapter provides the keys that will open the

way for understanding, insight, and wisdom, rather than confusion and constant bewilderment. Understanding these three
elements is essential to produce a common bond of love and
acceptance in any broken relationship.

ANGER

Everyone knows what it is like to be angry. From time to time,
anger wells up inside even the calmest of individuals. Its seeds
are the minor irritations that fester and grow into resentment
or erupt into uncontrollable rage. Anger is no fun! It is the
emotion that has the greatest potential to put us out of control
the fastest. Normal folks look more like convicts or residents
of state mental institutions when they are angry than when
experiencing guilt or fear. When anger spikes in moments of
intense rage, the world must beware. It drives its victim to the
brink, and often over the edge into irrational behavior. It
makes for instant insanity. In its path there are usually many
hurt feelings and destruction of lives.

Anger on the rampage can be deadly. Many lives have
been taken when a fit of rage was accompanied by a handy
weapon of lethal capacity. The highways of California in
the summer of 1987 erupted into deadly violence at the
hands of angry motorists, out of control and with access to
firearms. An epidemic of freeway shootings plagued the
state as motorists feared that a traffic mistake might result
not in a ticket but in a warning shot from another driver or
a fatal bullet in the head. There were some incidents of ran-
dom thrill shootings; but the majority resulted from tem-
pers that could not withstand the heat of the California

freeway system combined with discourteous and thought-less motorists. Anger often kills when it is out of control. Woe to the man or woman living in the home of another angry person.

Anger not only leads to deadly violence when unchecked; it also kills in subtler ways. There are millions of drug addicts who are shooting up, snorting up, or washing down some chemical that will soothe the anger-ridden mind of the user.

Blood pressures can peak because of unresolved anger. Some scientists say that cancers grow best in a metabolism prepared by the chemical reactions produced by anger. And lives are wasted away in depression as the temper is left unex-pressed and turned inward. Anger is a thief that steals life from individuals and potential from relationships. And in its most destructive form, for both individuals and relationships, anger fuels a fire that burns up the will to survive. To extin-guish anger's fire, its main propellant must be examined.

EXPECTATIONS

The desire for external fulfillment. It is surprising to many that an examination of anger starts with expectations. The source of any expectation is the desire for external fulfill-ment. One without a desire for external fulfillment would be content to live in the jungle and live off the fruits of the trees. There is nothing wrong with the desire for external fulfill-ment. That desire, when combined with hard work, leads to accomplishment.

College degrees are acquired from the internal acquisition of knowledge and the external fulfillment of recognition for a task completed. Without external fulfillment needs, people would simply study until they had learned what they needed and then withdraw from school. The diploma motivates individuals to continue when the desire to go on is weak. In many other instances, the desire for external fulfillment or expectations are healthy elements of personal achievement. But often the desire for external fulfillment becomes distorted. When it comes without any work to obtain the fulfillment, or when the desire for what accomplishing a goal can produce, the path toward anger is laid.

When expectations become unreasonable and dreams are not fulfilled, anger is born. The unmet expectation is the source from which anger boils. Many people are disappointed—even ticked—when they realize life does not come with a book of guaranteed rules, a fairy godmother, or magic wands issued at birth that can be used to make dreams appear in an instant.

These people live as if they are angry because life does not magically work out the way they instantly want it to. And often that anger is played out in a disbelief in God. They want God to be the Divine Magician who will ease the hurt and assist in acquiring earthly gain. When it does not work out that way, when God refuses to be relegated to the role of a magician, the individual seethes with anger and pronounces that there is no God. This type of external expectation for fulfillment always leads to anger, disappointment, and the inability to continue to relate constructively with another person.

When expectations are unreasonable. Angry people in a love-hate relationship are always full of unreasonable expectations. And no human being could ever live up to those expectations. They live in constant tyranny of how things "should" be in a perfect world. Reality becomes too hard to accept, so the focus is moved onto "what should be" rather than "what is." And the "what is" of life is never enough to satisfy the desires of those with unreasonable expectations. Every time the perfect life is replaced with the natural and normal irritations of life, anger resurfaces to torment the individual and everyone else in the area. Rather than find some way to live comfortably within the environment of today, the angry person is involved in a futile attempt to control the environment. But this world will not be controlled and managed by a mortal. The more intense the attempts at control, the greater the disappointment when reality hits. The unreasonable expectation must be replaced with an acceptance of reality as it is.

In the case of the Blanchards, their anger was not at each other. At its root was the unrealistic expectation that they would go through life without tragedy. And when that tragedy hit, it hurt more and more with each passing day. The more it hurt, the more they prayed to God to heal their daughter and remove this nightmare from their lives. When God did not grant this wish, their anger increased. It was anger at God, but it was expressed toward each other.

The hope for their relationship would rest in their ability to see their disappointment and focus on the other person's need for help and strength during that difficult time. Their expectations were unreasonable, but that was not their only problem. They also were experiencing the loss of a dream—the dream that their daughter would change and give them some grandchildren.

When dreams don't come true. When expectations are lost and dreams die, anger results. Angry people are trapped by those who do not meet their expectations. And since no one can meet those expectations, everyone becomes a trap that immobilizes each angry individual. The dream, that thing that is believed to bring instant happiness, is the bait in the trap. And angry people always go for the bait, never for the person. Angry people do not engage in relationships; instead, they go after what the relationship is supposed to bring. That product might be money, success, fame, or eradication of misery—all part of the contrived dream. And when the other person does not deliver the dream, rejection and bitterness are the natural outcome.

Angry people lose the willingness to forgive the other person when their expectations and dreams do not materialize. This egocentric existence is full of people who bring misery rather than an instant solution. Every person is seen as a source of hope for instant relief. But it is always false hope that can never be accepted. That is why so many single people fake true love in the beginning of a relationship, only to discover that the object of that love will never deliver the dream. Then the only course of action is to bail out of the relationship as quickly as possible. What appeared deep and intense was only a superficial search for an unrealistic dream.

And angry singles full of unrealistic expectations never forgive others for being human. They just move out and on to another person in hopes of finding what others seem incapable of understanding. Eventually that person is left with reality—a very lonely reality that just will not do. Anger explodes from discovering reality and being unwilling to accept it.

In the case of many happily married couples, their anger develops at the onset of some crisis or tragedy. When they determine that the marriage or the children are not going to materialize magically like in the movies, they become angry. Rather than move on like the single person, they often stay, but with bitterness and resentment toward the partner. Then they become involved in behaviors that are wrong because they feel "justified."

An affair feels OK because the other marriage partner is blamed for failure. There will be no forgiveness granted for unmet expectations because as long as there is blame, the unrealistic and angry partner believes there is reason to go outside of the marriage for fulfillment. Thousands of marriages end because of this phenomenon, but few husbands or wives understand what has taken place. When dreams do not come true, rather than allow anger to separate and divide, love can allow for the creation of new dreams. But angry people must be willing to forgive the world for not being a place where dreams always call for pleasure and personal comfort.

When I cannot meet another's expectations. There is another side to the anger-expectation connection. Rather than coming from others not meeting my expectations, anger comes from the inability to meet another's expectations. An easily identifiable example of this is when a person is raised in a home full of rigid standards and religious rules. These strict parents leave no room for negotiation about behavior. The children interpret that certain behaviors make them good and certain behaviors make them bad. They do not see themselves and the behaviors as separate entities. They do not grow up believing themselves to be of worth, although capable of evil. They view themselves as evil unless obtaining approval for their actions that someone else desires.

These children of perfectionistic parents often grow up trying to meet expectations that are far beyond anyone's ability to achieve. This constant failure to produce destroys self-esteem but also fosters continued attempts to live up to someone else's expectations and the search for someone who will say, "Well done." This fruitless existence makes for a very angry individual, churning and boiling on the inside but appearing like the perfect person on the outside. After all, to display a negative emotion might produce disapproval from another person. This internal anger will be resolved only when these individuals stop seeking approval from others and accept themselves as creations of worth from a God who loves them.

RELEASING THE ANGER TRAP

No one walks out of the anger trap without resolving his or her expectations, without lining up his or her expectations with the reality of the world. Others cannot deliver an impossible dream. And when that dream is not delivered, the people who fail to provide it must be forgiven for their mortal limitations.

Nor can the individual continue to try to live perfectly within some superhuman standards. This self-inflicted tyranny must be replaced with self-acceptance and the realization of God's love and acceptance. Resolving this negative emotion of anger is a vital part of taking the hate out of the love-hate relationship. But it is not the only emotion to be resolved. Fear and guilt must also be managed.

FEAR

If anger results from others not fulfilling our dreams, then fear comes from the belief that others will create for us a

nightmare. Anger is much more directed toward what someone has done than is fear. Fear is directed at the other person's
ability to create some unknown danger that lurks out there in
the distance. In love-hate relationships, the other partner
comes to be viewed as the facilitator or cause of that future
disaster or tragedy. Often this exceptionally difficult relationship results from our seeing ourselves in others. We do not
like what we see in them because we know it also is in ourselves, and we fear that we will become more unlike who we
want to be. Rather than accept our own ability to change or
be in control of who we are or what we do, we project that
onto the other person. This causes more fear of the person
and enlarges the hate dimension of the love-hate relationship.

It is ironic that in our fears of the other person, we give to
that person powers that they do not possess. We are in control,
but we fear that they will control us. We pull back from the relationship out of fear of being trapped within it. Rather than save
us from something, this fear tears us from what was or could be
a loving relationship and thrusts us into a destructive pattern of
giving and then running. If we do not run to another person, we
stay; but we stay at a distance, observing and calculating each
move of the other that would justify our own fears.

Rejection, out of fear, replaces acceptance, out of love. And
the love-hate bond than grows stronger. In most instances
there are two basic fears that must be handled to disengage
fear. Those fears are the fear of being abandoned and the fear
of being smothered.

ABANDONMENT: THE FEAR OF BEING LEFT BEHIND

The issue of trust. There are countless numbers of relationships that never start because one person refuses to trust the

other. Behind this lack of trust is the belief that if I commit myself to the other person, that person will take advantage of me and abandon me. The fear is that the abandonment would be painful. I might discover that life is not safe, that I am not in control of all circumstances, or that I might not be able to survive the rejection that comes with being abandoned. Perhaps there was an earlier instance of abandonment that I do not want to relive. Thus I flee for another superficial relationship in which I know I will be in charge of my own destiny and especially the destiny of the other person and in which I can feel secure that if anyone does the leaving, it will be me.

A similar occurrence happens within marriage. One partner starts to see his or her own inadequacies and weaknesses, especially in times of crisis and struggle. Rather than accept them and trust that the other person will accept the imperfections, that partner zeroes in on the inadequacies of the other person. This is a vain attempt, an unknowing exercise to rid the fear of abandonment. In essence, I make the other person appear inferior and incapable of leaving.

It is a device to maintain control. The more I point out the other person's faults, the more that person will realize I am wonderful and he or she is fortunate to have me. But rather than develop allegiance, this unconscious exercise only serves to drive the two further apart.

Once again the Blanchards' discord is an example of this dimension of the love-hate relationship. As their daughter's illness grew more debilitating, more painful for everyone, each of them felt more and more to blame for their daughter's impending demise. Unconsciously fearing that the other spouse would determine the future death was the fault of the other, each one began to tear at the other's self-confidence.

This was mutually self-defeating as both of them wore each other down. It was a maladaptive form of preservation, with each becoming willing to do anything to avoid blame from the other. The cycle would have been broken instantly if either one of them had asked the other, "Do you think that this whole ordeal is my fault?" Each one could have reassured the other that there was no fear of rejection or abandonment. But instead, they, like many others, avoided the confrontation and in the process avoided helping the relationship.

The needy person. Instead of refusing to trust anyone out of fear of abandonment, some people tend to latch on to others so that they will not be left behind. Like a hungry parasite, they sink their teeth into the other person until they cannot be removed without great pain to the host. These hangers-on come to define themselves in terms of whom they are hanging on to. They sacrifice their own identity to become just like the object they love.

Or they become like a nonexistent human being who is nothing outside of the identity of the stronger spouse. These people often wake up around the age of forty, miserable and unwilling to just exist. This new awareness causes great grief in the marriage as the former needy person asserts the real need to establish an identity.

But many needy people never realize what has happened to their own life and individuality. And they become incapable of living alone. The thought that they are completely dependent on someone else repulses them. They will do anything not to think about what would happen if the other person died or left. They can't stand what they have become, but they feel powerless to stop the way they are living. Either way they are saturated with fear, afraid of being left, or afraid of a worse abandonment. They become afraid that they will abandon themselves forever and never become an independent creature. Motivated by fear, the needy person repeats the mistakes of the past and enhances and increases his or her fears with every new situation and relationship that is mishandled.

Coping through separation of emotion. The fear of abandonment leads to another reaction, different from distrust or the development of a super-needy personality. This coping process is called separation. Rather than resolve feelings of anger or resentment, the person in this mode merely separates conscious thought from those feelings. This, like the other coping processes, occurs out of fear of abandonment. The person avoids confrontation so the other won't leave him or her stranded. The result is very damaging for the individual.

In separation, a child might resent or hate the parents. But rather than express feelings of anger toward them, the child separates from those feelings and becomes extremely wonderful when the parents are around. The child will refuse to acknowledge or act upon the hurt or fear that is felt and will separate those feelings out as if they did not exist. A facade of false emotion is constructed to give the appearance that everything is wonderful.

At this point, the individual has withdrawn from the relationship. There is no potential for it to grow because of the hiding of real feelings. Many think that not expressing feelings is the Christian thing to do. But in reality it kills relationships and robs people of their potential. The relationship goes no further than that point at which the separation occurred.

The child who separates emotions out of fear of abandonment exemplifies what it is like to love and hate someone at the same time. There is the traditional love and respect for the parent, but beneath it is a contempt and hatred that forms the real foundation of every interaction. That child is likely to grow up determined not to be like Mom and Dad. The standard gets set at whatever Mom and Dad are. But rather than pass beyond that standard and excel into unique individuality, the child stumbles into becoming just like the parents. We really do become what we think about, and with the aid of some strong genetic influence, the person turns into a carbon copy of the parents. There results a symbiotic fusion between the parents and child, each locked into roles they cannot escape because of the unwillingness to honestly face up to the emotions they feel.

Abandonment of self out of fear of abandonment. The fear of abandonment takes on many forms: becoming distrustful, becoming too needy, or separating from feelings. Each of these unique forms of adaptation to the fear actually increases the fear rather than resolves it. As the fear increases, the degree of anger and hate in the relationship increases. Eventually the relationship is destroyed. The result may be perpetual discord or divorce, but it is never healthy. And the world that is created from this fear is a very insecure place to live.

The secure person with solid self-esteem does not react from fear. That person relates out of love and acceptance. A natural flow of emotion can take place in a relationship because there is no survival mode in place. There are no desperate attempts to cope with a situation. There is mutual trust and respect that allow each individual to grow and expand into greater human beings. The one becomes the fertilizer for the good of the other while maintaining a strong sense of worth and identity.

The love-hate relationship, full of fear, does not allow the healthy part of the individual to grow or the unhealthy part to heal. Instead, the unhealthy part is nurtured and what was strong within the person is made weak and impotent. The fears drive the person into inappropriate reactions that are self-destructive. The best choices are passed over for poor decisions. In this process, the individual is lost. The person who could have existed is lost in a morose mass of confusion and fear. That accumulation of emotion so handicaps the person that abandonment from other people becomes more likely.

Few, other than the mutually unhealthy, want a relationship with a person who is full of fear of being left behind. The unhealthy who are able to stand it for a while cannot maintain the energy needed to cope with this type of desperation. It is only a matter of time until the person is abandoned, just as he or she had feared.

When the abandonment finally takes place, the person is left without a relationship, without love, and without self-esteem. The greatest loss is that of the person. Out of fear of being left, the individual betrayed him- or herself and ended up with little left to move on to another relationship. When that occurs, the struggle to survive can only be more desperate, more tainted, and much sicker than before.

THE FEAR OF BEING SMOTHERED

The opposite fear of being abandoned is the fear of being smothered. It is the extreme apprehension that someone wants to smother my identity and my unique qualities. It is the belief that if I am not careful, the person with whom I have a relationship will totally erase who I am in favor of who he or she is. My struggle becomes one of self-preservation. Often this fear is based on the fact that there is someone who actually does smother. Many times this fear is generated by exposure to an unhealthy mate or parent or boss who acts in such a way that all freedom is dissolved and individual autonomy is destroyed.

The act of smothering is frequently an offshoot of the person's fear of being abandoned. The smotherer is or was most likely in a relationship that either dissolved or was under constant threat of breakup. In an unhealthy attempt to survive and cope, the person clings to another person so tightly that smothering occurs. The actions of this controlling parent or spouse or boss lead the other individual to extremes to survive within the relationship. But often the smothering process is so complete that although the other person wants out of the relationship, he or she is unable to get out. If the smotherer had resolved the fears of abandonment from the past, there would be potential for a healthy relationship. But until that is done, there will be a lopsided affair with one clinging on and the other struggling to break away.

A sad but all too common example of this smothering process occurs with divorce or with the death of a spouse. A mother, left with a teenage son, may resort to some smothering techniques toward the son out of a fear of being left behind again. So she may be overprotective, withhold privileges, and demand the boy be with her rather than with his friends. He may not be allowed to play sports out of her fear that he will get hurt and die. She may even take him into her bed, holding on to him since there is no one else to hold on to.

For the child, this becomes a terrible burden, and all people are viewed as threats to personal freedom. That smothering relationship with the mom provides the fear that all other women would do the same if given the opportunity. So solid relationships do not develop because the boy is afraid of getting involved in a smothering situation again.

THE CHAIN OF MULTIGENERATIONAL MISERY

The two fears, fear of being abandoned and fear of being smothered, are integral parts of a love-hate relationship. And they feed into each other. The person who fears being abandoned is likely to smother whatever is closest. And the person being smothered is likely to fear that others will attempt this smothering process. He or she will become overpowering in the relationship in an attempt to exert control and prevent smothering. This is likely to result in the other person's developing unhealthy fears and the inability to develop normal relationships. Thus, the mantle of unhealthy fear is passed on from one generation to the next. Fear is bred throughout the family and passed on to the next unhealthy generation. The normal is replaced with the abnormal and reproduced with the development of each new relationship.

The only hope is that one generation will break out of the rut and become free from the predictable misery that is experienced by each new family that is formed with love-hate dynamics. Resolution of fear is the only hope for a transition into healthy relationships full of love and without hate.

GUILT

The third destructive emotion that is found in the realm of love-hate is guilt. The Blanchards' problems with their own relationship were increased because each parent experienced extreme guilt over their daughter's lifestyle and her development of AIDS. Guilt drove a wedge between them like it does between others who allow it to enter and control a relationship. This is why the Christian marriage has so much more potential than non-Christian marriages. The Christian has forgiveness modeled in the form of Christ's sacrifice on the cross. The Christian is taught to forgive seven times seventy times, symbolizing that forgiveness should be a never-ending process of allowing each other to start over. That does not happen in the love-hate relationship. In that relationship the guilt is compounded with blame from the other, until self-condemnation becomes unbearable.

THE LIFE OF THE "IF ONLYS"

One of the most stagnating forces for the guilt-ridden relationship is the negative thinking pattern of "if onlys." This repetitive thought process is close to unbearable to live through and extremely unbearable to live around. Regret is the central form of expressed and unexpressed feelings. The regret is for things that "I" did not do and things that "you" did not do. These thoughts and regrets are compressed into feelings that are internalized and buried. The internal self-depressing statements go like this:

If only I had made better decisions.
If only I had been brought up in a better family.
If only I had married someone else.
If only I had spent more time with my children.

When the feelings are expressed and projected onto others, they are expressed like this:

If only you had not been so stupid.
If only you had lived up to my expectations.
If only you had made more money.
If only you had not failed to understand our child.

This "if only" thinking takes all of a person's energy and emotions and uselessly spends them on a destructive, repetitive rehash of the past—through the dank marshes of what might have been. This focus is so all-consuming that anyone involved in it is without strength or motivation to resolve the past and move on to achieve a future full of possibility. It is a game of a loser who is satisfied to give up at a tough place rather than move on to another challenge. Being stuck in the past, wandering through all of the maybes of life, robs life from individuals and relationships. Those weighed down by these thoughts need to move on and start working toward maturity again. Otherwise, all that is achieved is an intensified love-hate relationship with yourself and with others.

The "if onlys" are not too distant cousins of the "its." Some forward-thinking people mainly believe that the accomplishment or attainment of some "it" out there will solve all problems. They believe once they "get it," everything will be wonderful. Fill in the "it" with a man, a woman, a car, money, a job, a position—any goal will do. But these forward-thinking people soon learn that there is no one thing that is going to change the entire world. No one item can provide the resolution for many complex circumstances in a very complex world.

The same concept applies for "if only" thinkers. No one thing, exercised differently or handled better or undone, would have reversed a complex history of a relationship or a human being. A child who might have avoided drugs could have become pregnant. A parent without money now might have lost it if he had it to begin with. A problem solved in one area of life could have produced others in another area of life. It simply is a worthless exercise to retrace the indelible steps of the past, trying to determine which better path would have led to happiness and fulfillment. The exercise itself plunges all relationships into no-win arrangements where misery compounds itself on the hate built for each person of significance. It is simple to see that relationships stuck in the past and nailed down by worthless "if onlys" cannot survive in the present. They die from hatred of others and self-contempt.

GUILT LOCKS ME INTO THE PAST

The "if-only" thoughts are an easy way to lock yourself and your relationships into the past but there are others that are just as destructive. Some do not think in "if only" terms; that becomes too simple. It also involves concluding that life could have been better if different.

Some choose a more intricate and consuming form of misery. These people choose to relive all the disappointments of their past. Each unmet expectation is dissected into hundreds of saddening pieces, each piece revived into consciousness and relived, piece by very sad piece. The patterns of the past invade the brain so that disappointment and regret are always in focus. Painful enough when experienced alone, each disappointment's pain is magnified as it is added to the pain of all other disappointments.

THE PRESENT AS AN ALTERED PAST

Reliving disappointment after disappointment forces behavior patterns of the past into the present, and the past is altered and recreated into a present form, lived out to provide future and greater disappointment. Because the person is unable to fix the past, a similar situation is subconsciously brought back in some form. The wife of an alcoholic gets a divorce and finds another alcoholic to marry. A child of an alcoholic grows up repulsed by the smell of liquor but falls headlong into a relationship with an alcoholic or drug addict. The unbearable past becomes an unbearable present, a repeat performance of a programmed disaster, no pain being too great to be redone.

Why does this happen? Why can't the person pull out of the mess? Why does life become a never-ending task of creating love-hate relationships? It is simple. The root of the problem is never uncovered and resolved. That root is unresolved guilt.

The guilt stems from an irrational acceptance of blame for a past addiction, divorce, or failure of any kind. The guilt forces the guilty to pay for the crime, and to pay and pay again until finally the guilt is made impotent through forgiveness of self and others. All that is necessary is a will to live in the pain long enough to discover that you could not have made things better or cured the sickness. Once this is accomplished, either instantly or through a long recovery process, the tormented victim can finally be freed from the past to begin a livable future.

GUILT LOCKS ME OUT OF THE FUTURE

Repeating errors of the past does not go unnoticed by the people who repeatedly trip themselves on yesterday's failures. It becomes obvious that every new opportunity and every new relationship has a snag, more like a snare, that hangs these people in past problems. So, naturally, a large amount of apprehension starts to dominate them. The guilt retains the focus on the past, guaranteeing the repetition of failure. Thus, fear of the future is bred out of that guilt. Those who are paranoid, full of anxiety, apprehensive at every junction of life, should look more at the issue of guilt than at the emotion of fear.

The guilty, absorbed in the guilt, are afraid of further damaging their lives and the lives of others with more mistakes repeated from the past. They fear that the result of hard work on new opportunities will only multiply disappointments. They often refuse to move beyond a narrow path of comfort. They stop trying. They stop achieving their goals or caring about whether or not they have any. They become drained of all motivation because of the fear of more failure, more pain, and more complication. Their guilt drags them down and slams the doors to the future in their depressed and isolated faces.

In addition to this intense fear that prevents the development of a future, there is another guilt factor that locks out the opportunities ahead. This comes from a preoccupation with reshaping the past. So much time is put into restructuring the past that there is no time left for the creation of the future. A woman looks for another irresponsible man whom she just might be able to fix this time. A man cannot give his grandchildren all that they deserve if he continues to try to make one of them into the ideal son who rebelled against him. A father cannot give his children pure love and devotion if he is still trying to reshape his own father into the man he never was. All of those energies are focused worthlessly on efforts that produce nothing if accomplished. They also create more guilt because of the neglect of the current needs of the family and the lack of attention given to future needs.

All of this manipulation of people, these tireless efforts to reconstruct the past, forces the person to become more and more controlling. In fact, the effort to reconstruct the past combined with the fear of further hurt drives the person to control every possible aspect of every possible situation. The greatest fear becomes the dread of being out of control. The person turns away from the future rather than preparing to enter it. When the future is considered, it is avoided because it cannot be controlled. The fear of the unpredictable, the fear of the unknown, the fear of a future beyond the person's means to endure and especially control—those fears drive the person back from the future. And those fears are born out of guilt from the past that remains unsettled.

GUILT LEAVES ME WITH A MISERABLE PRESENT

Guilty people are miserable people. And they are full of excuses for that misery. Life becomes so crummy, so irreparably bad, that the obvious excuse is rendered: "Who could have done any better in my circumstances?" Reality becomes so unbearable that the guilty person finally gives in to the self-imposed sentence that will be doled out over a lifetime. That unconscious payment for the guilt will be made day after miserable day with no attempts to change, just a resignation to the fact that life must be this way. In place of action to resolve problems, there is left only inadequate excuses to try to explain away the miserable consequences of an irresponsible life that never included the painful experience of working through the problems of the past.

Another frequent excuse of the guilty goes like this: "How was I supposed to get over what I had been through?" This excuse focuses on the past being locked in and its misery being unavoidable in the present. It reveals the underlying feelings that at one time I might have been able to do something about the problem, but since no one helped me then, since I was not rescued at the point when I could have been saved, there is no hope for happiness now.

A person with this belief pattern under the surface is so full of guilt and resentment that any relationship with that person would have to contain a large amount of hate and bitterness and anger. It makes the person the ideal candidate for a love-hate affair that could last a lifetime. And it will last a lifetime until the person realizes that excuses only delay recovery from the problem and produce more pain than the original source of the problem. These people must turn away from justifying why they are undeserving victims and move into a new phase of accepting responsibility to change themselves. If they remain in the victim mode, excusing their circumstances because of the problems they were up against, they make victims of everyone involved in a relationship with them.

CONCLUSION: BREAKING UP
THE LOVE-HATE FOUNDATION

Fear, anger, and guilt form a solid foundation for every love-hate relationship. These emotions evolve in a predictable pattern in most of the people who are in destructive love-hate situations. That predictable pattern or cycle works as follows:

1. *Fear.* Unresolved fears of childhood and adulthood produce in me a helpless belief that the world will never be a safe and wonderful place for me to live.

2. *Anger.* The helplessness that I feel from all of my fears leaves me angry because I feel inadequate to remake the past.

3. *Guilt.* My failure to remake the past produces within me a feeling of guilt because I refuse to forgive myself and others.

4. *Results.* So I struggle through life, unable to relate as a healthy human being, involved in multiple love-hate relationships that I never resolve.

This result is a subtle phenomenon in the lives of many. Their relationships contain no knock-down, drag-out fights. There may rarely be a harsh word spoken between the two people involved. But there is death within that relationship. There is no true communication, no sharing of the feelings that are troublesome to each other. This allows two seething and resentful people to go separately through life although they may rarely leave each other's sight.

There is a better way. Life does not have to be such a terrible, lonely place. There is hope for change. But on the way to that hope there is pain in breaking out of those old patterns that have locked in the love-hate dynamics. But once the decision is made to go through that painful experience, the love-hate foundation of fear, anger, and guilt can be destroyed and replaced with love, hope, joy, and freedom.

Chapter Three

THE RESULTS:
LIVING WITHOUT A ME

WHEN I AM UNABLE TO RESOLVE THE LOVE-HATE RELA-
tionships in my life, I can only survive by denying who I
really am and creating a false identity to hide behind. This
loss of my real identity can begin early in my life; or it can
be the result of my reaction to some severe emotional
trauma that I experienced later in my life. To understand
how this occurs, the best way is to look at how it happens
early in my life.

THE LOSS OF ME

When an infant is born, he or she enters a strange and hostile
environment. Prior to birth, every need was met without any
waiting. Following birth, life is different: Now I experience
changes in temperature. I experience hunger. Lights are bright,
and all kinds of people stick their faces in front of me. In

41

God's plan, He provides a person called Mother whose main task now is to meet my needs as best she can. Since I cannot talk—I can only cry—her task is not very easy.

As the months pass, I begin to experience frustration. Sometimes I need my diaper changed, and instead Mother gives me a bottle. Sometimes I just want to be held, and what I get is a bottle propped up next to me. Sometimes I cry and Mother doesn't come, so I end up crying myself to sleep. Since my world revolves around me, I begin to wonder what I am doing wrong to cause my frustration.

As I continue to grow, learning to walk and say a few words, I find that Mother really enjoys what I do. Sometimes she spends a lot of time with me, laughing and playing with me. Other times, she hardly seems to notice me. Or if I touch something, she yells at me and hits my hand. That hurts, so I cry. I begin to experience the world as having good parts and bad, painful parts.

In my infantile way, I struggle to understand where the good belongs and where the bad belongs. Because my understanding of the world is so limited, I begin to think there are two categories—good and bad. I think that Mother is good, because most of the time she takes care of me. That leaves only one place for the bad to go—me. My world consists of Mother, who is all-good, and little me, who must be all-bad. This understanding can be diagrammed like this:

Mother———————————————————all-good

--- split

me———————————————————all-bad

THE IDEAL ME

As I get a little older, I keep trying to do things just right so that I don't experience any pain, frustration, or disappointment. I gradually bury the real me, which I believe is all-bad, and begin to create images of me that I show to other people. These images include my achievements and successes—anything that gets me approval from those around me. As I do this, I am developing a false me, or an ideal me, that I show to everyone around me, hoping that they do not ever see the real me. As I grow, I spend a lot of energy keeping this ideal me out where everyone can see it. It may take the form of a perfectionist, a caretaker, a high achiever, the "best little child around," or any combination of these and other facades that reflect our ideal. This propensity can be described like this:

Facades of the Ideal Self

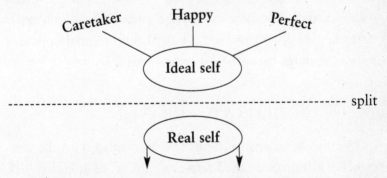

I have to keep the real self buried as deep as possible, because I am convinced that that part of me is all-bad and totally unacceptable. What I bury with it are all the painful emotions that we discussed in chapter 2. But as I get older, it becomes more and more difficult to keep all those painful emotions buried. They keep coming to the surface, destroying that idealized picture of myself that I so desperately want everyone to see and love.

As these painful emotions keep coming to the surface, I come to the point where I can't cope any longer with the badness I feel within, and I begin to externalize these feelings and project them onto someone else in my life. Usually this focuses on the person with whom I have the love-hate relationship. If I can blame someone else for the bad feelings I have within me, then I will be able to strive to be the ideal self that I have worked so hard at becoming.

But when I start blaming, I become overwhelmed with guilt. I feel torn between the "love" feelings and the "hate" feelings I have for the same person. When I am feeling love toward him or her, I hate myself and feel worthless inside. When I feel hatred for that person, I am filled with guilt; but at least then I feel as though there is some goodness within me. Eventually I become torn by the inner conflict I am experiencing. As I do, my real self is buried deeper and deeper, and my real feelings become even more hidden.

DEFECTIVE GRAFTING

In an effort to escape from this endless conflict, I can become involved in a process called *defective grafting*. In order to break out of the destructive cycle described above, I find someone to "rescue" me. I discover the perfect person to relate to. This person is everything I want to be, and if I can somehow connect with this person, I will be able to break free from my love-hate cycle.

My "knight in shining armor" comes along and sweeps me off my feet. He or she is absolutely wonderful. I have met the ideal person! I want to possess that person and be possessed in return. That person represents everything that I have ever wanted to be. (The absolutes used in this paragraph are not an exaggeration of the intensity of these initial feelings.)

Rhoda was trapped in a love-hate relationship with her mother. All of her life had been spent trying to win her mother's approval—all to no avail. Her mother is controlling and intrusive. When Rhoda was a teenager, her mother would take it upon herself to cancel Rhoda's dates if she felt uneasy about either the boy or Rhoda's attitude. Often her mother would follow her places to observe her behavior. When Rhoda protested, her mother insisted it was all done because she "loved Rhoda so much."

Rhoda was trapped in her feelings of love for her mother, since she obviously cared a great deal for Rhoda, and her feelings of intense rage and hatred at being controlled by this intrusive person. Rhoda wasn't allowed to think for herself. She wasn't good enough to do so.

When Rhoda met Larry, he was a dream come true. He was the "white knight" who would rescue her from the intrusive, controlling, and belittling parent. And anyway, at age twenty-five, Rhoda was ready to get away from home. Three months later, Rhoda and Larry ran away to get married. Rhoda was in paradise. She "lost herself" in Larry. It was all so romantic, so freeing, and so idealized. What Rhoda couldn't do by herself—break away from her mother's control—she could now do because of Larry. She "grafted" herself onto him as her savior.

What Rhoda didn't realize was that her real self was still

buried. What she longed to accomplish through her relationship with Larry was not possible, for she lacked the inner sense of self that would provide the stability she longed for in her marriage. And since she had Larry so idealized, she really didn't know the person she married.

Not long after they were married, Rhoda discovered that Larry was intensely jealous of any attention shown to her by anyone, even by her girlfriends. He began to monitor her activities and limit her contact with friends. Within a year or two of their marriage, Rhoda felt as if she was living in the same prison she had experienced with her mother. She felt victimized by the person she had "grafted" herself onto.

This is an example of defective grafting. In her relationship with her mother, Rhoda was unable to establish any sense of a real self. That pattern was repeated in her relationship with Larry.

Why would people want to graft themselves onto someone else? Why would Rhoda repeat the conflicts of her family life? For one thing, Rhoda experienced a period of time when she felt free of the harsh, critical parent, from both without and within. Remember, the conflict with her mother was most severe *within* Rhoda. Mother's influence, critical attitude, and distrusting spirit were all internalized within Rhoda. By the time she was an adult, she didn't need her mother to be present in order to create a conflict within. What is often called the *punitive superego* was always present. That is, it was present until Larry came along and provided an escape from it all. But, as is always the case, that relief didn't last, for eventually Larry became just like Rhoda's mother.

During that period of relief Rhoda experienced, she also

felt as if she had escaped from that inner sense of badness that had plagued her all her life. Larry made her feel worthwhile, like she was a person. Unfortunately, that was all part of the idealized fantasy—that all was now okay. All Rhoda did in reality was create another false self to cover up the emptiness and emotional pain and conflict.

VARIOUS FORMS OF DEFECTIVE GRAFTING

Defective grafting takes place in other ways as well. Sometimes people go on an active search for someone to "graft" onto and lead very promiscuous lives. They are looking for the ideal person, and sex is the area of their search. The disillusionment and victimization in one relationship only leads them on to another object to graft themselves onto.

Often people who feel empty in their marriage relationship find the "ideal" person outside their marriage. This person of their dreams suddenly appears and an affair begins. The fantasy often includes the idea that they can have both—they can keep their mate at the same time they explore the "wonders" of this idealized person who has mystically entered their life. It's only after the affair has ended and they attempt to pick up the pieces of their lives that they realize they have been victimized by defective grafting again.

Sometimes the affair doesn't end; the marriage does. And the person rides off into the sunset with their ideal—another one who will rescue them from the agony of not knowing themselves. They were unable to resolve their conflictual feelings in one relationship, so they graft onto someone else who promises an instant solution.

Sometimes the defective grafting is not onto another person; it is onto a thing, like a job, money, or an activity. Ron was trapped in the quest for more and more money. He was already worth more than most people will make in a lifetime, but it wasn't enough. In his mind, Ron felt that if he could just achieve a net worth of several million dollars, he would be satisfied. Then his idealized picture of himself would become real.

Several years ago, Ron had reached that figure; but now it "wasn't enough." He had to revise the figure upward. In the process, he lost his marriage, spent very little time with his children, had several superficial relationships, and worked every minute he could. He had several love-hate relationships in his life. But as long as he was "grafted" onto his quest for that illusive figure of net worth, he didn't have to deal with his own lack of self and his internal conflicts.

Others "graft" themselves onto alcohol or drugs as an escape from who they are and what they feel. Sometimes food is a "better" addiction, and they eat in order not to feel. The pattern of eating and purging, called *bulimia*, is a symbol of the love-hate relationship. These people desire food or nurturance. But as soon as they eat, they feel a hatred toward that food and must purge themselves of it. They can't decide whether they want to eat or purge, love or hate.

Defective grafting is a destructive process that feels good at the beginning. It's the end that destroys us. Sometimes the result is a serious physical illness, such as ulcers, colitis, migraine headaches, or even cancer. More and more research is showing that a high percentage of serious illness finds its root in our internal emotional conflicts.

People trapped in love-hate relationships can become very

violent in their other significant relationships. The helplessness they feel leads to an inner rage that spills over into violent behavior. The violence only intensifies and perpetuates the conflicts within. The rage leads to guilt, which produces more rage, and then more guilt. The more trapped these people feel, the more they find themselves trapped in the bitterness of their own souls.

Sometimes the conflict can be so intense that people report they are going crazy. Love-hate relationships involve loyalties that run deep. We've worked with people who would rather give up their own sanity than come to terms with the truth of their love-hate relationships.

People who are victims of defective grafting often reverse the role and become the caretaker of the person who has grafted into their life. Rhoda chose this as the path of least resistance. The more Larry attempted to control her life, the more she became his caretaker. She fell into the same trap that she had with her mother. She believed that if she could just be a good enough wife to Larry, he would act differently.

As an adolescent, Rhoda had firmly believed that if she would get good grades, do things for her mother, and be the "perfect" child, Mother would finally approve of her and give her the acceptance she so desperately wanted. In reality, all she ended up with, with both Mother and Larry, was the job of taking care of them. The love and approval she sought were never to be found.

Sometimes people who are trapped like Rhoda become accident-prone. It's as if they have accidents to punish themselves for not being able to resolve the dilemma. This isn't a conscious process. It is an unconscious reflection of their lack of self-acceptance and lack of self-appreciation.

So much of the defective grafting process sets people up for repeated victimization, both for themselves and for their children. The syndrome then is passed from one generation to the next. All we can do is cope.

Chapter Four

---∽∞∞∽---

How People Cope with Love-Hate Relationships
(Achieving Temporary Results with Negative Decisions)

IT IS NOT EASY TO LIVE IN A LOVE-HATE RELATIONSHIP for an extended period of time. In fact, it requires some very complicated and refined coping skills to do it. The problem is that too many people are able to develop these means of coping. So they just go on, day after day, coping with the situation. Either they are unaware that they can do more than cope, or they are unwilling to do it. Those resigned to merely cope with the situation are not happy people. They are in need of a motivation implant. Whether they stay in the relationship or leave, they render themselves powerless to change. They lose faith in the power of God to change the situation. They give up on prayer as a means to facilitate change. They cope without hope.

HOW TO STAY RESENTFULLY INVOLVED

Jake Sanders was an unusual fifty-five-year-old man. He was the mayor of a small town in Georgia. He had power and prestige that came with being the most famous person in the city of ten thousand people. He had been responsible for the fruit-growers co-op that provided buying power to the small farmers in the area. He had rebeautified downtown with plants and trees and flowers that would have made Lady Bird Johnson weep with appreciation. His own Ford dealership just at the edge of town was credited by the company as selling more Fords per capita in a one-hundred-mile radius than any in the country. He had more plaques on his wall with little gold Model Ts than just about any Ford dealer in the land. His motto was simple: "If it has wheels, we will figure out a way to sell it to you."

Jake made things happens. And because of it, he was the biggest fish in the small pond of Shambley, Georgia. His wife of over twenty years, Rebecca, was not content to live in his shadow. She had her own life as part of Shambley high society. Her efforts had turned the vacant O.K. Grocery building into a library that everyone in town was proud of. Because of her efforts in raising money, the former produce section was now a resource center for young learners. Where soap once had been displayed, the periodical section now existed. And where people once had bought their meat, they now looked over the current bestsellers. She was a make-it-happen person in her own right. In Shambley, the Sanderses were people to be admired.

Jake and Rebecca seldom missed a Sunday at the First Baptist

Church of Shambley. Jake would always smoke a Camel before going in to teach his Sunday school class, but his teaching was superb. His rationalization of smoking was that if it was the worst thing in his life he ever did, he wasn't so bad. Then he would add that since it was not the worst thing he ever did, there was no use in giving up the smokes until he cleaned up the rest of his act.

The church had been a place for the Sanderses' children to grow up with a strong faith in God. In town they were known as good kids. There was Jenny, the oldest, and Jeremy, three years younger. Jenny was a brilliant girl who had gone on to graduate from Yale and had moved to Atlanta, working her way into the top management spot of an investment firm. She had a strong husband, a committed Christian man who loved her greatly. All was in good stead with her life. It was her brother who was the "black sheep" of the family.

Jeremy resented everything about his father that everyone else admired. That his dad was wealthy and powerful was of little significance to him. He felt that his childhood had been mortgaged to acquire that wealth and power. All he had wanted from his dad was time, affection, and love. What he felt he had received instead was a nod here and there and very little love or affection. It had been hard living up to the Sanders precedent set by Jake, Rebecca, and his sister, Jenny. He had the brainpower, but besting them seemed to be a rewardless endeavor. Even to *match* their accomplishments was an overburdening challenge. And his father was too busy with the town affairs, too busy with Fords, and too busy with the church to help Jeremy with the dilemma of facing an insurmountable problem: the fear of being a total failure. It was that fear that led Jeremy into a life that could be characterized as a total failure.

Jeremy pumped gas at the gas station on the corner of the town square. The old Sinclair station had become his stage to wear his badge for suffering within the Sanders family. He did not run to another town; he did not even pick a job of isolation and obscurity. He stayed in Shambley and worked where almost everyone could drive by daily and shake their heads at the "lost potential" who pumped gas on the corner of Main Street and Georgia Avenue in downtown Shambley. He was punishing himself, and he was punishing his dad. He could not give up paying the price for feeling he had been rejected as a child. He accepted no responsibility for his life and felt that he had been the ultimate victim.

Needless to say, Jake and Jeremy had few kind words for each other. Every week they had Sunday dinner together, and almost every Sunday they fought, argued, blamed, questioned, and probed into the misery they caused each other. It was not a pleasant situation. And Rebecca, feeling helpless to make things any better, always wondered why it had to be this way. She wondered why two people who hated each other so much had to live in the same town. Why did they have to eat at the same table? Her desire was for Jeremy to move on to another place. She felt that if he did, he might start over and find happiness that up until then had escaped him. She was very puzzled at the whole arrangement of the father and son, so bitter with each other yet so closely woven into each other's life. They defined what it was like to be resentfully involved.

MOUNTING AGGRESSION

Not only did Jeremy choose to stay resentfully involved with his dad; he chose to do so in an aggressive form. His expression of resentment in the love-hate relationship was blatant. He attacked his father, not only with the open display that he had not met the expectations of the world or developed even one-half of his potential, but also verbally. He pointed out everything wrong with his town. He made sure that Jake knew all of the sins of the members of the First Baptist Church. If there was something negative to bring up, Jeremy seldom passed up the opportunity.

There had been a time when Jeremy had made attempts to reduce the hostility between the two. But the harder he tried, the angrier he became. The frustration mounted each time he heard his dad say something that brought up a resentment from the past. He did nothing more than transform himself into a raving twenty-year-old child who was destined to continue to fight with his father. He could not see that the battle could not be won. He failed to recognize that his fighting only prevented him from accepting responsibility for overcoming the problems of the past. Rather than moving beyond the childish spats that he created over and over again, he relentlessly pressed for some ultimate victory that was never to be won.

In this situation Jeremy was trapped in with his dad, neither could ever win. He certainly was not going to win by fighting battles that increased his resentment. And just at the age when Jake was ready to enjoy slowing down and relaxing into semi-retirement, his son was a constant strain on his life. He was losing days and years that he would never regain, while the constant stress shortened his life. Yet in a very sad way he was responsible also for the continuance of the tyranny, born out of his neglectful fathering. At any time he could have stopped the struggle and asked for forgiveness or simply approached the subject of Jeremy's childhood in a way that proved he was interested in resolving the issues of concern. But instead they both continued to press against each other at every turn, not changing course, not changing their minds, not trying to reach each other beyond the conflict. All they did was try to develop new tactics in the fight that held them both captive.

HOMEOSTASIS

The family system of the Sanderses rested securely on the tip of a very unhealthy balance point. The longer they continued in the vein in which they were relating, they greater the groove at the balance point and the less likely that anyone or anything could topple the system. Each person fit in the relationship at the point where the balance could most easily be maintained. Dad allowed Jeremy to come over and berate him day after day. Mom still prepared a Sunday dinner for the family even though it was nothing more than a forum for expressed contempt. And Jeremy continued to go there and start the dance of malcontent that he had performed for most of his life. No one *had* to come to dinner. No one *had* to stay in the same town. And any of the three could have upset the sick balance by deciding to change, get help, or work toward forgiveness.

There is a reason it did not work out that way, that no one changed and no one made an effort to change. They were locked into the agonizing relationship with all of its pain and misery. They did not do anything to change the fighting, because once the fighting stopped, no relationship would be left. Out of the context of struggle, these people had nothing to say to each other. They did not know how to say things to each other except for a superficial report on the day's events. But because of that internal drive to belong and relate, some relationship became better than no relationship. And the struggle continued between father and son, aggressively attacking each other, fighting to win the destruction of the other. All this was done in a vain attempt to cope with a situation that was left unresolved from years gone by. Their method of coping did not lessen the pain or change the reality of the family. It left them torn, hurting, and without hope.

PASSIVE COPING

Unlike the Sanders situation, many people choose passivity over aggression in their attempts to cope with a love-hate relationship. Rather than confront and attack, the passive person sits back and stews. The hurts and disappointments go unexpressed, and these feelings expand each day they are repressed.

Most people have seen this type of situation, where a woman is married to a jerk and she copes with this by becoming a passive "doormat." She would rather lie at his feet like a lap dog than mention that his feet are dirty. She exemplifies the destructive character of the passive person and how rolling over and playing dead can be even more destructive than aggression.

The doormat spouse lives an existence that its totally non-confrontational. Anything is acceptable if it prevents confronting a problem in a way that might prove painful. She is fearful that she will be the victim of her spouse's rage, that she might be abandoned or isolated. So she plays out her role, always being the loser. In fact, she becomes the perfect loser. The husband, experiencing failure at work, compensates for his lack of power there by exerting total power over her. And she learns to be the perfect target for his displaced rage. She learns to respond by taking it all in and still working to make him feel more comfortable.

She may have been taught by her mother that it is her wifely duty to respond in that way. As long as she is willing to absorb the brunt of her cruel husband's fury, he will continue to use her as a way to rid himself of the frustrations of his business life. Then, in a moment of guilt, he will retreat from his overpowering ways and seek to make up by lavishing his wife with gifts and kind words. This reinforces the behavior, making the beatings and shouting worth it because of the prize that is offered at the end of the episode. He needs big help, and so does she. She is part of an epidemic of enabling that can be stopped only when she wises up and seeks gratification other ways.

Over time, the bad becomes much worse, and the rewarding moments of repentance become less and less frequent. The doormat spouse realizes that there are no real rewards in a relationship of this type. But rather than confront the issue, she sits back and waits for the impending failure to occur. In fact, she uses passive-aggressive behavior to spur the failure on. When she notices problems, she refuses to reveal them to the husband. Messages are forgotten about and important information is not communicated, all in a subtle and often unknowing attempt to produce the failure as quickly as possible. The adverse effect of this strategy is that before the mean spouse loses, the doormat is lost—sometimes forever.

The mistreated spouse loses self-esteem and feelings of self-worth. They are lost because of the demeaning treatment. But they are also lost because of the awareness that she has allowed herself to be treated in such a demeaning manner for so long. These feelings of low self-esteem and outright disgust can so depress the person that psychiatric treatment is the only way to pull him or her back from total self-annihilation. The painful life is out of control, and if the person does not commit suicide, she might just choose escape from reality with alcohol and drugs.

It is not a pretty sight when the doormat wakes up to the situation she has created for herself. It is a crucial time that could mean recovery or self-destruction. The doormats of today must look beyond their present circumstances and see what the outcome can be when they continue to live passively in a love-hate relationship. They must wake up to save their marriages and to save themselves. And whether that doormat is male or female makes no difference. No one should live at the unloving mercy of another.

THE OPTION TO LEAVE

The other option in the love-hate relationship is, of course, to leave. It is a method used by many to cope. Those people who are too afraid to confront or too hopeless to try to make the relationship work opt out of the partnership rather than struggling with ways to cope with the situation. This method is more hopeless than when the person stays, although not productively, but stays until perhaps he or she stumbles on a way to resolve the hate in the situation. But those who leave take with them all of the hope for a renewed relationship. They leave only to latch on to another relationship that is the same in nature, just a bit different in form. Left behind is a trail of broken, unresolved relationships, each one more painful than the last.

RETALIATION

Coping with the process of leaving presents many difficulties, which are blamed on the other person as they increase in their inconvenience. There is resentment over the treatment endured while in the relationship, and there is resentment from the aftermath of the separation. To cope, the individual who leaves, now experiencing new freedom, plots to retaliate against the person who is at the center of the pain and disruption. This retaliation can be found in trying to turn a child against the other parent or withholding that child from visitation. These power plays are daily nightmares in divorces in which custody is up for grabs. It is certainly not the picture of peace and serenity that was expected when the separation began.

Children leave home in an effort to cope with the heartache that is generated by unloving parents. Often children head for Hollywood in search of their dreams—only to find bad dreams on every corner. The child believes that leaving will solve all problems. It does not. The child is also more than willing to put the parent through as much worry as possible, in an effort to retaliate against the childhood that was taken away. This is a classic example of an attempt to hurt someone else that ultimately produces greater hurt for the one who is retaliating. Leaving home proves to be worse than staying in the relationship, seeking professional help, and requesting assistance in dealing with the difficult parents. But for most rebellious kids, leaving presents the prospects for freedom for themselves and punishment of and retaliation against the parents.

DISPLACED RETALIATION

Frequently the retaliation is unknowingly displaced onto others not involved in the love-hate relationship. Some go out and retaliate against all society. This is seen in public shootings, suicide plans with bombs to kill others simultaneously, and other types of socially deviant behavior, such as stealing. One of the worst forms of this displaced retaliation comes as child abuse. The child becomes the victim of the rage that is produced from leaving the love-hate relationship. Unable to strike out at the true culprit, the parent victimizes the child through all sorts of abuse. In addition to children, the elderly are also the recipients of cruelty. Whoever the victim, the displaced anger destroys the world and robs the next generation of the security that they need. This most maladaptive method of coping needs to be stopped by anyone who is aware of its existence. There is no excuse for allowing an abuser of others to continue.

PROJECTION

Another form of coping occurs when the separated persons project their problems onto others. They cling to others who are unhealthy; this provides an excuse to exist in an unhealthy state. They marry the same type of troublemaker as before to try to prove that they were not the cause of the earlier trouble. When questioned about their negative circumstances, they always have the other unhealthy person to blame. This coping mechanism provides the excuse they need and lets them continue the

victim's role. The victim searches out and clings to the victimizer, who becomes the perfect target for projection of the
problem. If the source of the problem is no longer around, the
projective person can always find someone else to play the role
of victimizer, someone to continue the cycle of defeat.

LEAVING QUIETLY

The last way that people cope with the love-hate relationship is
to leave quietly, not retaliating and not projecting the problems
onto others. They are determined to hold in their feelings, live
with the hurt and pain, suffer through it, and deny that anything is wrong. The stress from this coping decision is so great
that the person seeks seclusion because one more source of
stress might put them over the edge. They become phobic of
other people, fearful that each encounter could be the one that
sets off an episode of being out of control. Their silence appears
to be admirable, but in reality it is as destructive as the other
methods of coping. In essence, the person ceases to be.

People who leave silently without expressing the true
feelings they are experiencing eventually split away from
those feelings so they do not feel the hurt. They become
superficial people others find impossible to draw close to.
They are always seeking ways to leave a relationship, to
find solace in their separateness. And all the while they continue to play the role of perfect survivor with no problems.
They place a lot of space between themselves and others,
and it is a rare instance when anyone can get close. That
usually occurs when life becomes so sorrowful that nothing
but a gallant rescue will help the situation. But those sought-
after rescues do not happen in most cases. The silent ones

just continue to bemoan their situation only to themselves, cutting off the rest of the world and their own potential to live successfully in it.

THE LAWS OF COPING

All of these coping mechanisms will work, but only for a while. Eventually each method leads to one of three outcomes:

1. death

2. insanity

3. resolving the conflict

Anyone can die; anyone can go insane. But it takes courage to decide there is hope in resolving the conflict and resolving the pain. It is helpful to get on that track as soon as possible. The sooner it occurs, the less pain must be endured and the fewer people will be hurt. There are only three options because of the two laws of coping:

First law of coping: Your mechanism of choice will always become less effective over time. That is why it always takes more and more booze, more and more food, more and more excuses. The coping mechanism dissipates in its effectiveness, and you must compensate for it, choose another coping mechanism, or decide to change.

Second law of coping: The adequacy of the coping mechanism will always decrease in proportion to the increase in intensity of pain. You may cope for a while, but as the pain starts to increase while the debris of your life piles up, you find that your coping mechanism malfunctions. It never meets the test in the face of great pain. Many sufferers choose suicide when the pain gets too great, or they combine coping mechanisms like alcohol and drugs, prostitution and eating, and other things that never produce a positive outcome.

So there are two enemies of everyone's coping mechanisms. One is time, and the other is pain. As time goes on and as pain increases, no coping mechanism can stand up to the task of helping you survive. That is why there are the three outcomes of death, insanity, and resolving the conflict. But the misery that drives you to the brink of death and insanity is also the force that invites you to change, get better, and start over. Once you eliminate that option, once you are determined never to take it, the other two will occur much faster. The only thing that holds back the prospects of death and insanity is the prospect of change and the hope of a better life. The better life is not one of merely getting by and coping; it is one of abundance and fulfillment.

Chapter Five

⊸∞∞⊷

BEYOND COPING:
OVERCOMING AND RESOLVING

TO COPE APPEARS TO BE THE GOAL OF THE MASSES—HERDS of people, all living in a day-to-day struggle to get by. They just want to survive, hang on, and hang in there. Their existence is the opposite of the abundant life Christ calls us to. John 10:10 says that Christ came to give us life to the fullest, the abundant life. Coping is far from life to the fullest. The mission of the "copers" is to white-knuckle their way through the pain and hope that someday, somehow, relief will come. But they eventually discover that they cannot run fast enough, talk long enough, drink enough, or do anything enough to enjoy life as a mere "coper." But there is another way to live. It is a better way. Its method is painful at first. But the gratification from this way of life is long-term. The results come from a determination to stop coping and start resolving the conflict of love-hate in your life.

ACKNOWLEDGING THE PROBLEM

MOVING OUT OF DENIAL

Jeremiah 17:9 states that the heart is deceitful above all things. Its very nature is dishonest. In other words, how you feel about things will trick you, because within yourself is the capacity to deceive yourself. How many people can you point to who go through life denying serious problems that cause great discomfort? They appear blind to the realities of a bad marriage, poor parenting, and other relational obstructions. They choose to let the gnawing agony remain long-term rather than experience short-term pain in order to resolve the conflict forever. These people are difficult to understand but very easy to spot. In fact, we can become so absorbed in observing their peculiar means of existence that we avoid facing up to our own peculiarities. We need to abandon our looks of scorn and focus on the man or woman who stares back from our own mirror. When we take the spotlight off others and turn it on our own problems, we move out of numbing despair and into a new realm of hope for personal growth and development.

It is not a unique practice to cover up problems rather than resolve them. Denial prevents the totality of our emotional despair from crashing in on us. It allows us to bite off the problems in chunks small enough to be more easily tolerated. But for most, laziness and procrastination prevent going back and uncovering the truths and resolving them. A state of denial prevents a sharp personal pain from surfacing, but it allows for and causes more pain over a long period of time. Denial never stops the pain. It numbs it temporarily, but it will not kill it.

Often a child will not forgive a parent for an emotional hurt or early neglect. The bitterness and hurt stay with the child because he or she denies the need to forgive the parents. Since parents are idealized creatures, their children do not want to admit that forgiveness is needed. They cannot accept those parents as less than perfect, even though they harbor deep-seated resentments toward them. All of these confused thoughts and emotions play together to prolong the painful act of total resolution. They all work together to fuel the denial of a need to act. And in doing so, the denial forces the person to repeatedly experience personal pain that grows deeper over the years. It is not a sharp, piercing pain but rather a prolonged, aching pain that comes from a broken heart and a hurting soul.

To move out of this denial mode, one must realize that there is pain. Our twenty-first-century shuffle keeps us so busy that it prevents us from taking the time to analyze our feelings and explore the regions of our discomfort. Eventually and individually we reach that point where we realize that our feelings are not the way they are supposed to be or have to be. We come to realize that we are going in the wrong direction, that today has more discomfort than the days of months past. Once it is accepted that something is wrong, then we can do something to correct it. But if the twenty-first-century shuffle just keeps you scurrying from place to place, you will not stop long enough to feel and to know that you really do hurt deep down. You will not realize that the hurt and pain are causing you many other problems as you try to compensate for their presence. Denial is the first step to not taking another step. Instead, stop and listen to the rumblings of your heart that are keeping you in constant turmoil.

Once pain has been acknowledged, you are ready to discover its source. The source of the problem, the person with whom you are engaged in the love-hate relationship, could be one of many people in your life, both past and present. A very likely candidate is a parent, but not necessarily the parent you cared for the least. It is probably the parent who looked the best or appeared to be closest to you. It is probably not the parent you openly despise, if there is one. It most likely is the parent or both parents you speak of most fondly. Your parents may be high on the love scale in your mind and also high on the disappointment scale. Your pain will come from the stronger parent because of the feeling that he or she did not do enough to help save the weaker parent. It takes time to identify the source, and it can be a confusing process. So it might be best to obtain some guidance or counseling while sorting through the source of the pain. In that process you may discover that the parent actually has little to do with how you feel. You may find that a brother or sister, a boss or employee, or your spouse is at the core of the conflict. The important thing is to start the search for the cause of the pain. Stop the denial by determining to discover the cause of your discomfort.

DISCOVERING THE FACTS FROM THE PAST

A friend of ours was involved with a family in which the grandfather molested one of his granddaughters. Lisa did not talk to her grandfather for years because the issue had not been resolved between them. Her cousin Sheila finally asked her why the two did not talk. After much prodding and encouraging, the issue of molestation was revealed. Sheila was startled. She had no idea that something like that could have happened in their family. As the days went by, Lisa's revelation to Sheila produced greater and greater amounts of discomfort for Sheila. She lost sleep and stopped eating. As you might have surmised, some very painful feelings were starting to surface as flashes of memory broke through her conscious thinking after being blocked for years. She began to mentally recreate the past that had eluded her for so long. The source of her discomfort became apparent. But there were gaps that she could not fill. So she began to talk to cousins, aunts, and uncles. Even with people she did not trust, she probed to find the secrets of her past. And the more she searched, the more she uncovered a sick man who had made many little girls his victims. The evidence of the problem was overwhelming, but it convinced her of two things. One, that she was not guilty, and two, that something needed to be done to help herself, her cousin Lisa, and her grandfather.

REALIZING THE NEED TO ACT

Action is the key to resolution of problems. Sheila not only decided to get help for herself; she decided to get help for her grandfather. She knew there was a risk that he would go to prison. That was hard for her to accept. It increased her pain. But even more troubling was the chance that there might be other victims. So she went headlong into a process of resolving the problems of her past while assisting others in facing theirs and moving to correct some wrongs. It was not long before she felt a tremendous weight lifting from her heart. There was a new freedom in her spirit that made her grateful for the chance to start over with feelings of concern where hatred had taken root. Her acknowledgment of the problem led to a wonderful outcome that never would have happened if denial had persisted and closed off her opportunity to deal quite successfully with the reality before her. She was well on her way to completely resolving the conflict.

CONFLICT RESOLUTION

There are some helpful lessons to be learned from the cousins and their abusive grandfather. They provide an example of how to correct a problem from the past. The initial steps that Sheila took are vital to resolving conflicts, stopping the lingering pain, and moving into a new realm of freedom. A review of her steps can provide a guide for others who experience pain from a love-hate relationship.

1. IDENTIFY THE PROBLEM

Others like yourself may be unaware or unable to accept that a problem exists. By defining it, showing its root, and amplifying the impact of the problem, you go a long way toward solving it. And in the process you may help others discover their part in the problem, their responsibility, and their need to take action.

2. IDENTIFY THE SYMPTOMS OF THE PROBLEM

If there is a problem, there will be evidence. That evidence is found in the symptoms that surround the conflict. These symptoms are very clear if you look for them. But they are invisible if you remain in the denial mode. There are many symptoms, and each love-hate relationship is a unique combination of interactions, but here are five of the most common symptoms:

• *One-sided communication.* In love-hate relationships, communication is not an equal exchange of ideas. It is not a mutual sharing of emotions, thoughts, and beliefs. Instead, every conversation has a winner—and a loser. The victor and the victim may exchange places from time to time, but generally there will be tension during each interchange until the winner has established the winning point and the loser has wilted into self-inflicted defeat, too hurt or sad to reply.

In parent-child relationships in which love-hate prevails, the child, although a grown person, is never allowed to communicate as an adult. The conversation always becomes a lecture, and the lecture is always a destroyer of self-esteem. In actuality, it is the lecturing adult who is without self-esteem and must maintain the dominant role so that no one discovers his or her low view of self.

There is no honesty in these one-sided conversations. There is intense fighting for position and complicated one-upmanship, but with little regard for reality. This type of relationship will continue until one person refuses to continue it. One person in the duel must finally say that there is no use in continuing the senseless game. That point can lead either to the beginning of resolution or to another symptom—isolation or withdrawal.

• *Isolation or withdrawal.* The natural result of repeated one-sided conversation is the withdrawal of one of the members into some form of isolation. This is why early-teen pregnancies or runaways occur in many instances. In a marriage, it results in divorce; in a job situation, there is either a firing or a resignation. But these overt means of withdrawal do not take place in the sickest of situations. In the worst cases, the individuals continue to live together or work together, but the victims withdraw into themselves, living in a lonely hell without expressing feelings, thoughts, or dreams. These spouses, children, or employees seem to be lifeless; they appear shy and unwilling to interact with anyone. Or if they do interact, it is with the least communication possible. Those who withdraw into themselves seem to be suffering because they are. And most likely they suffer from the third set of symptoms, which are psychological in nature.

• *Psychological symptoms.* Guilt, anxiety, and depression intertwine into a labyrinth of mental and emotional distress. The victim often cannot point to the direct emotion or feeling because he or she vacillates between anxiety, fear, and the depression that results from the anxiety—anxiety over the fear that as bad as things are, they may become worse. Guilt over nothing—but over everything—accompanies the anxiety and depression to overwhelm the person and prevent dealing with the emotions. The victim is so confused, so hurt, that the little effort that could be extended is not; it seems to be too futile, with too little resources available for too great a problem. So the person, vacillating in and out of emotional interludes, struggles along in his or her own private world where no one appears to care and no one is allowed to know that they care.

• *The inability to say no.* Deluged by emotional overload, isolated and withdrawn, depleted of inner strength, the victim in the love-hate relationship loses the ability to say no. Then the tyrant in the relationship has free reign over the victim. Sexual favors or perversions are dolefully carried out with little effect, even though the inner pot of emotions is on high boil. Whether the victims are spouses or children, they lose the ability to fend for themselves. Actually, they lose their identities and find themselves as an extension of the tyrant in the relationship. Without the assistance of a knowledgeable friend or family member, there is a chance this subservient lifestyle will continue.

• *Repressed awareness of pain or hurt.* This was discussed earlier but is mentioned again because it is so hard for the victim to accept that what is felt is real pain, real hurt that is not experienced by others and is demanding to be addressed. When the repression stops and the expression starts, new energy is acquired to deal with the other emotional terror that is lived out every day. It is vital that the victim see this natural tendency to repress pain as a reversible process that can lead to healing. The fear of the surgeon's knife is similar to the fear of facing up to the pain that is being repressed. But in finally allowing the pain to surface and be felt, like the surgeon's knife, the painful procedure to remove the offending problem and move into healing can begin.

3. CONFRONTATION

Life without confrontation is a life without risk lived in fear of what others can and will do to me. But confrontation does not have to be a disaster that leads to one person punishing another. It does not have to heat up a situation. It can be an effective tool to cool down and change the rules in a love-hate conflict. Confrontation is a loving act done for the sake of both parties involved so that each person can get out of the love-hate trap and into a free and meaningful existence.

When the problem is identified, when the symptoms are clarified, it is time to work on the art of confrontation. And the better prepared you are to execute that art, the better the outcome and the greater the opportunity for emotional healing. Following are some guidelines that provide the greatest chance that confronting a person in a loving way about the faults in a long-term relationship will help turn that relationship into a strong and positive one, even after years of hurt.

• *Avoid blame.* Pinning the blame on the other person will most likely shut down the resolution process. And there is no reason to blame. Most likely the other person is well aware of his or her wrongs and has done many things to compensate for the guilt. Although the other person might have been the perpetrator of the sick relationship, it takes two people to make a relationship work, and it takes two people to make a relationship continue to work poorly. Rather than nail down the wrongs of the other person, you want to motivate that person to change. Stating what was done wrong will only strengthen the defense process and cause the battle to heat up. Sentences that start with the word "you" usually end with blame toward the other person. They are to be avoided in a productive and loving confrontation.

What is important in a confrontation is that each person comes to realize that there have been some inaccurate perceptions. The other person's perceptions of how you feel have been inaccurate because you have stopped trying to express yourself and reveal your emotions. You have agreed to behaviors that you despise, so the other person has felt justified in continuing the behavior. The only way to rectify the problem is to express how you have felt, tell how you want things to be, and reveal your desires in a realistic and sincere way. Allow the other person to know you from the heart. When you do that, you avoid blame and allow the defenses to be lowered. That provides the greatest potential for a successful confrontation.

• *Express your personal needs.* In expressing your needs, realize that the other person may not be able to meet those needs. You will have greater success if you initially tell the person that you have needs and that you realize that some of them may appear to be excessive or too much to handle at this time. While you realize that your needs are not wrong, you are allowing the other person to consider them excessive while he or she becomes accustomed to the fact that you not only have these needs but have expressed them and expect something to happen because those needs have been made known. You can use words like "I wish . . ." and "I want . . ." to begin your need statements. This avoids blame and positions you to say exactly how you feel and what you need.

• *Request change.* The reason you are confronting is because you want things to be different. You expect some action that will lead to change. You are changing rules that have been hard and fast for a very long time. This will cause the other person to feel pressure. And pressure to change is a tremendous force that is always met with some degree of resistance;

so when you request change, you must do so as subtly and positively as possible. Never make a demand. After a long and sick relationship, this is no time for an ultimatum. This may have to come later, but allow the person time to consider you as you have revealed yourself.

Be specific in your requests, but always allow for alternatives to the way the request can be fulfilled. Your request may be that in order for the relationship to change, you would like for both of you to see your pastor to discuss some problems. The other person may want to see someone more detached or remote than your pastor. Realize what a positive move that would be and maintain your flexibility. You may even want to ask for ideas from the other person on how the situation could be fixed. If a stagnant relationship starts to move even a little, your confrontation will have been successful. It is then your job to keep the other person motivated toward continuing the movement. If you remain flexible and open to the alternatives, the other person will not be overwhelmed and will not refuse to take the first step.

• *Confront only behavior.* If a specific behavior that must be confronted, such as alcoholic drinking, there are some guidelines to follow when you must bring up specific actions. Remember that it is the behavior, not the person, that you are confronting. Any behavior you bring up must have been witnessed by you. It cannot be secondhand information or hearsay. You must not get trapped into confronting a person for someone else or confronting a rumor rather than a behavior. Only use instances that you have witnessed firsthand or participated in. Otherwise, the person will feel unfairly attacked and the defenses will increase, causing more trauma for the relationship.

The confrontation can be a wonderful event for both people. It can break you out of your silent hell and give you new freedom. For the other person it allows a way out of the rut or trap that has been created in the love-hate relationship. Often the person being confronted feels the most relief because he or she did not want the situation to continue on the same path either. The success of the confrontation has much to do with your preparation and attitude. If either is poor, it is best to seek help in providing an opportunity for change through confrontation.

When Moses came down from the mountain and the Israelites were worshipping a golden calf, he did not love them into a new way of acting. He did not merely pray for change. He confronted them and obtained the change in behavior that was needed. When Jesus entered the temple full of money changers and overturned their tables, he was expecting change in behavior. He did not take a passive or weak stance with those people. He did not patiently stand by and wait for them to decide what they were doing was wrong. He confronted the behavior and set the example for us not to just hope and pray. There are times when the most Christian or biblical thing to do is to take action with a loving confrontation.

4. ACCEPTANCE

Confrontation of behavior alone can be a dangerous thing. It can cause a relationship to reverse its imbalance, remaining just as unbalanced but in a different form. For a person to go from a doormat to a raging confrontational bull is a terrible mistake that few people could tolerate. The ability to confront behavior must be tempered by the willingness to accept the other person.

• *Move beyond perfectionistic expectations.* As our ability to get in touch with neglected needs increases, so does our level of expectations of the other person. We can become trapped by a growing tendency to expect perfection from him or her. Then that person may start to feel that the more that is given or changed, the greater the demands will be. Seeing the expectations rise above the ability to perform, the person may decide to dig in his or her heels and not move beyond the troubled stance of love-hate paralysis. The confronter must understand this and, in a patient attempt at compromise, be willing to give up on a position of absoluteness. Yes, you may have been deeply wronged, but you are not perfect. You do not have a corner on goodness. See your own faults and imperfections so that as you confront you can also accept more and more of the person you do not want to hate.

• *Focus on the positive.* Few people in our generation do anything without motivating encouragement and positive reinforcement. Be sure that as you confront negative behavior, you take the time to uncover the positive aspects of the person and the relationship. Even a sick relationship with a perverted pedophile will contain some positives to reinforce change. There is nothing better than encouraging behaviors you want developed and then affirming those positive behaviors when they occur. This provides for the balance needed to see positive change take place. In addition to this, when you minimize negatives, you create an even greater force for change. Avoid saying, "Yes, but . . ." to statements; this is one way to ensure that you are not becoming picky and overbearing. Overbearing people will win many small battles and lose the entire relationship in the end. Do not allow yourself to get into that mode; it is self-destructive and ravages any potential for the relationship.

• *Allow others to be human.* No one is going to be perfect. And no one is going to be consistent in the relationship 100 percent of the time. Do not overreact by viewing minor setbacks as major failures. Give people room to stretch themselves and then temporarily contract back to more comfortable ground. Small failures are part of the human dilemma, and responding with acceptance can provide added motivation to regroup and continue on the path toward healing the relationship. In allowing the little failures, you move beyond the temporary breakdown of the process, which, if complete, will move from acceptance of the person to forgiveness of past misdeeds.

5. FORGIVENESS

This is the big one. Everything that gets better between two people in a love-hate relationship does so because both people are willing to do this wonderful thing for each other. Forgiveness wipes the slate clean; it removes the bugs from the roots of the relationship. It unbinds the wings of freedom so that each person in the relationship can flee the past and acquire a future full of love and acceptance. It is not a small act. It is an effort of major proportion. Its effects are not instant. Only after repeated reassurances of forgiveness does the person start to move in his or her own power.

• *Ask for it.* The best way to give forgiveness is to ask for it. After a confrontation, nothing is more motivating and healing than for a person to say, "Now I want you to forgive me for my imperfections and shortcomings. I want you to forgive me for failing you." Defense barriers are bludgeoned when humility seeps in to allow a request for forgiveness to get out. The lines of communication are opened, and there is hope for renewal.

• *Change your focus.* When you forgive a person, you commit to improve yourself while you allow others to work with God on their own deficiencies. This takes the criticism off others because you become so busy working on yourself that you no longer have time to work on others. And when you do see others' faults, they only serve as reminders of your own problems that you are working diligently to solve. This change in focus allows you to begin the exciting process of living your own life. And it frees others from your scrutiny so that they can improve at their own pace that will produce lasting change.

There is a story of two monks who had vowed to avoid all earthly temptation. This meant no contact with anyone of the opposite sex. It was a lifelong vow that had to be carried out over decades. One day as they walked back to the monastery, it began to rain heavily and the streets became quite muddy. As they approached one street full of puddles and mud, a young girl stood there in her beautiful kimono unable to cross to the other side. One of the monks went over and picked her up and carried her to the other side of the road. The monk accompanying him was stricken with anger. They walked in silence until they approached the monastery. Finally, the monk could contain himself no more. He reminded the other of his vows and asked why he had carried the girl across the road. The monk replied, "I put her down back there on the road, but you seem to still be carrying her."

So many of us are carrying others' baggage, the dirty laundry that they have long ago resolved and forgotten. We must forgive them and allow them to move on and celebrate their act of starting over. We must focus on the future together rather than allow each other to be haunted by the past. We must let go as we allow others to let go. In so doing, we develop an entire lifestyle of forgiving. We plan to forgive. We look for instances when we can forgive, and we forgive again. Seven times seventy is not too many times for us to let go and allow God to mend the past and reshape the future. As we do this, we are able to recommit ourselves to each other day after day and year after year.

6. RECOMMITMENT

Recommitment is the final step in the process of resolving love-hate relationships. It is so important because it occurs when the warts and blemishes of a person's character are fully exposed. Anyone can be committed to an idealized conception of a person: a young child to a parent, or a new bride to her husband. But when the relationship has gone sour, the flaws have been revealed, and there remains a commitment, it exemplifies what Christ has done for us even as we have repeatedly betrayed Him. In recommitment, there are no surprises. The reality of the individual's character has been fully exposed. And when that character is revealed and accepted, good and bad, it is a wonderful experience for the forgiven and the forgiver. As the recommitment continues, the depth of forbearance and perseverance grows also. Each person knows that unconditional love has returned. And that love grows each day, as each person recommits love, acceptance, forgiveness, and growth to each other.

CONCLUSION

The resolution of the love-hate relationship is a tremendous act of growth for both people. It becomes part of a larger plan to grow and mature in wisdom. Patience comes from the process. The rejector has no patience. The one who crosses the barriers of personal weakness becomes strengthened. And where bitterness soured life, gratitude now sweetens it. All because one person refuses to live in misery any longer.

As growth continues, the boundaries of self are strengthened as self-esteem rises. Places of safety and confidence are found. The act of giving becomes more commonplace. New areas of discovery are explored as two people accept each other's weaknesses and build each other up so that the strengths that exist can be fortified. New confidence comes to the relationship as each person strives to find happiness in pleasing the other.

When these elements are put together, a relationship can then stand the tough times. As problems snap at the foundations, like a snake striking behind glass, you eventually learn that the strike will not touch you; the venom, though real, will not hurt you. The glass that protects you is a mixture of forgiveness, acceptance, recommitment, and confrontation. Eventually when the snake strikes, you do not jump, because you realize you are safe behind the barriers that you built together.

As a person heals one love-hate relationship, there is an urge to heal others. All of life's personal interactions have a chance to get better. Caring relationships are strengthened, and toxic relationships are avoided. Each person, once controlled by the sick bonds of love-hate, becomes a seeker of changing, dynamic relationships. Of course, the process does not work 100 percent of the time. But until you develop the courage to take the first step, you will never know whether or not by changing one sick relationship, you may begin to heal your entire world.

Chapter Six

———— ∞∞∞ ————

WORKING OUT
THE INNER RESOLUTION

MANY TIMES THE PROCESS OF CONFRONTING THE PROBLEM can feel as though it is even bigger than the problem itself. I can identify the problem, but I can't even begin to imagine confronting the person involved. That thought is even more upsetting than the problem itself. I am paralyzed because I can't even develop the desire to actually work through my love-hate relationship.

In this chapter we will be working through some personal exercises that will provide the internal structure needed to be able to work through love-hate relationships. It is important that you work through each exercise in order so they build on each other. Space is provided for you to write in this book. You may want to write out these exercises in a separate notebook since some of the exercises will require additional space for you to process all that you are feeling. We encourage you to take the time to work through each exercise.

EXERCISE 1: DEALING WITH DENIAL

For many of us, the love-hate relationship that has been developed with a parent or loved one has been replicated in other relationships in our lives with people we try our hardest to avoid. We don't like to be around them because when we are, we feel drained. These are people who always seem to trigger within us a determination that this time we will not be set off by them. We *will* get along with them. But inevitably we end up in a minor or major conflict with them. Often the other person is not even aware of the struggle we are having—but we are aware of it! Often it feels like we are being parented by these people, and we end up feeling childish around them. Life puts these people in our lives, and try as we might, we can't escape them.

Take some time to think of at least five people in your life who would fit into this category. Write their first names below:

_____   _____

_____   _____

_____

After you have written down at least five people, rank them according to the severity of the conflict. You can do this by writing the number 1 by the name of the person you struggle with the most. Then write the number 2 by the person you struggle with a little less, and so on until all the names are ranked. (If you can't think of five people, write down as many as you can identify.) Now you are ready for the next exercise.

EXERCISE 2:
THE PROBLEM BEHIND THE PROBLEM

We have identified people in our lives with whom we have love-hate relationships. Usually these are people with whom we have strong ties emotionally but who have also deeply disappointed or hurt us at some time. It helps to identify these conflicting feelings. For each person on your list, fill in your feelings on a chart like this one:

Ways this person has disappointed me	Things I like about this person

As you fill in each side of the chart, you can see how you are pulled back and forth by the positive and negative experiences

you have with these people. The disappointments on the left
side of the column hurt you deeply, but you are drawn back
to the person by the likable qualities on the right side of the
column.

Now let's get a little more specific. Using the same people
on your list, fill out the following chart for each person:

Describe the last situation you can recall in which this person disappointed you.	What did you expect the person to do that he or she did not do?	List the feelings you had or have as you recall that situation.

When you have finished both charts, take some time to reflect
on what you have written about each person. What similarities do you see in your disappointments?

_____

_____

_____

What similarities do you see in the behaviors of the other people? How are they alike? How are they different?

_____

_____

_____

_____

What similarities do you see in your own feelings in response to the situations and the people?

_____

_____

_____

_____

EXERCISE 3: FACING WHAT YOU FEEL

As described in chapter 2, the unresolved fears of our lives cause us to feel helpless. This helplessness leaves us angry. If We don't know what to do with this anger, we end up feeling guilt as a futile attempt to remake the past. Since we can't work through these feelings, we stay stuck in the cycle, unable to find forgiveness for either ourselves or others. In this exercise, we want to identify the emotions we are feeling, especially fear, anger, and guilt.

FEAR

Let's begin by looking at fear. In each of the relationships we have been considering, write down all the things you are afraid of. For example, what are you afraid might happen if you changed the way you relate to that person? What are you afraid of losing? What is it that you have never had from that person that you are afraid you would have to give up hoping for? Write down these fears:

_____

_____

_____

_____

We are often paralyzed by fear without knowing exactly what it is that causes fear. Take each one of the fears you have identified and write out the worst possible outcome that would result if that fear were to come true:

_____

_____

_____

_____

Now go back over your list of "worst possible outcomes." Write down your estimate of the probability of each really happening. For example, you may have said that the other person would ridicule you or embarrass you in front of someone else. What is the likelihood of that happening? 20 percent? 50 percent? 90 percent?

When you have finished, look over the list of you fears and think of actions you could take to protect yourself from such an outcome. Write down some of the things you could do:

_____

_____

_____

_____

ANGER

We have seen that we experience anger when we want something from a person and are powerless to get it. With each of the people we have been working on, we are caught in a love-hate relationship because we want something we can't have. Finish the following sentence for each person on your list:

I am angry with _____ because he or she will not/did not

I am angry with_____ because he or she will not/did not

I am angry with_____ because he or she will not/did not

I am angry with _____ because he or she will not/did not

I am angry with_____ because he or she will not/did not

Look back over what you have written. Underline all the "shoulds" or "should nots" that you wrote. If you substitute the word "wish" or "desire," how does it affect the way you feel when you read what you have written? You might want to look back at chapter 2 to review the tyranny of the shoulds.

Identify some of the things you wish you could say to each of these people as an expression of your anger. Write down some of your thoughts:

_____
_____
_____
_____

GUILT

Often when we express our anger, we end up feeling guilty. Look back at what you have written about each person and answer the following questions:

Did your anger result in guilty feelings in this situation?

_____
_____
_____
_____

Did you feel guilty before, during, or after you were with this person?

_____
_____
_____
_____

Describe some of the "if onlys" you feel in relation to each person. (The "if onlys" are described on pages 32–34).

_____

_____

_____

_____

Look at each person on your list. What kinds of things do you do for that person that are motivated by your feelings of guilt? Write them down:

_____

_____

_____

_____

Look back over this exercise and circle the emotion that you feel hampers your relationships the most: fear, anger, or guilt.

EXERCISE 4: EXPRESSING YOUR EMOTIONS

Now that we have identified the problem behind the problem—along with the emotions you are feeling—we need to find a safe way to express your emotions. One of the best ways we have found to do this is to write the person a letter that you never mail. When you write a letter that no one but you will see, you can say anything you want—no holds barred.

It is very important that you express your fears, your anger, and your guilt in as clear and emotional a tone as possible. And it is also important that you do it without apology or rationalization. You are writing what you are feeling, and you have a right to those feelings.

After you have written your letters—which you may want to keep open-ended in case you want to add things later—let them sit for a while and then go back and read them. Keep them in a safe place where no one else will read them. When you are all finished with the process, you may want to have a ceremonial burning of the letters as a symbolic statement of your freedom.

EXERCISE 5: EXPECTATIONS VS. REALITY

We have worked our way through to a clear understanding of our feelings in relation to those people we both love and hate. As a result, we should be able to see these people in a more realistic way. Look at each person you have been working on and make a list of the expectations you have had for that person. In the column next to that list, describe the realities of the relationship as you see them:

My expectations for the relationship	The realities of the relationship

As you look at each list, are you willing to let go of the expectations and accept the realities? If not, you need to go back to your open-ended letter and express more of your hurt and anger. Your objective at this point is to be able to accept the realities and release your expectations.

EXERCISE 6: SEEING THROUGH THE OTHER'S EYES

This exercise requires the use of your imagination. It is based on your having done the previous exercise. If you haven't, this exercise will probably be too threatening to do.

In this exercise, you will try to see the situations you have written about from the point of view of the other person. Try to imagine how each person you have been working on might view the situation with you. What might be going on in his or her mind? Work through the following questions for each person on your list:

What are some of the personal struggles the other person has experienced in his or her life?

_____

_____

_____

_____

What feelings was the other person experiencing? You have to guess on this one, so guess all the possibilities. For example, was he or she frightened? Defensive? Hurt? Or something else?

_____

_____

_____

What motives might have been behind the other person's actions? For example, were they innocent? Unaware? Dealing with their own problems? Afraid? Intending to hurt you?

_____

_____

_____

Now go back over your lists and estimate the probability that each idea, feeling, and motive could be true. Write out a summary statement of how the other person might have experienced the relationship with you—from his or her point of view.

_____

_____

_____

EXERCISE 7: A COURSE OF ACTION

Exercises 7 through 9 assume the other person is still alive. Based on what you have experienced and learned from the previous exercises, take the time now to write out what you believe would help the relationship with the person you both love and hate. What would you say to that person? What are you willing to forgive? Where do you need to be forgiven? If forgiving is a problem for you now, write down when you think you will be able to forgive.

_____

_____

_____

_____

_____

_____

_____

_____

_____

_____

Determine a method by which your feelings can be expressed to this person. Will you write a letter? Make a phone call? Set up a luncheon meeting? Take someone with you? As you follow through on your course of action, it is important that you envision *both* of you being satisfied with the outcome. Write down what you will do:

_____

_____

_____

EXERCISE 8: A POSITIVE FOLLOW-UP

After you have worked through your action steps with the person or persons on your list, list two activities you could do with that person that would be enjoyable, safe, and non-threatening and pose a minimal risk of added conflict. List the two activities below next to each person's name.

Person #1_____   Activity #1_____
                            Activity #2_____
Person #2_____   Activity #1_____
                            Activity #2_____
Person #3_____   Activity #1_____
                            Activity #2_____
Person #4_____   Activity #1_____
                            Activity #2_____
Person #5_____   Activity #1_____
                            Activity #2_____

After you have finished your list, circle the name of the person you are going to call first. Then contact him or her, offer the two options you have identified, and let the other person choose an activity with you that would be a positive follow-up to the previous meeting you had. Again, envision a positive outcome for both of you.

After you have completed the activity, write your reactions below. Describe how the activity went in comparison to how you thought it might go.

_____

_____

_____

_____

_____

EXERCISE 9: SETTING SOME GOALS

Most of us look at relationships and operate under the idea that they "just happen." We seldom think of defining in concrete terms how we would like them to be. This is especially true in marriage. This exercise is designed to help you set some goals for mending your relationship with the people you both loved and hated.

To begin, use your imagination to envision your relationship with this person five years into the future. You can assume anything since it is the future. Imagine that the relationship is exactly the way you have always wished it could be. Write your thoughts about what that relationship would be like:

_____

_____

_____

What kind of behaviors by both of you would make it ideal?

_____

_____

_____

Look back over what you have written and describe two or three small steps you could begin taking now that would start that relationship on the path toward your ideal.

Step 1: _____

Step 2: _____

Step 3: _____

EXERCISE 10: THE MOST DIFFICULT
LOVE-HATE RELATIONSHIP

Probably the most difficult love-hate relationship you have experienced is with yourself. We are the hardest on ourselves. We know every flaw and failure in our past.

To help you work through these issues with yourself, go back to exercise 2 and list yourself as the person you both love and hate. Then work through exercises 2 through 6 with you as the focus. When you have finished, return to this exercise and complete the following step.

To finish this exercise, make a list of all the people you have harmed in the past. List their names here:

_____

_____

_____

_____

_____

_____

_____

Circle the names of those people on your list with whom you need to make amends. Number them in the order in which you are willing to contact them. If contact with any person on your list will compound the problem or hurt the other person, do not circle that name. Now, list below the names of those you are going to contact, in the order you will contact them. Then write down how you will contact them.

I need to make amends with . . .	To do so, I will contact them by . . .

Making peace with those in our past helps us resolve the inner discord we often experience with ourselves. Those who have taken the step to make amends with those they have hurt in their past have found it to be a crucial step in their own healing and growth. As you work through this last step, you will begin to create harmony out of that inner discord.

Chapter Seven

An Ounce
of Prevention

IF YOU WORKED THROUGH THE EXERCISES IN THE LAST chapter, you know how much emotional energy is involved in resolving love-hate relationships. We hope you found some resolution through that effort and are beginning to resolve those kinds of relationships in your life. In reflecting back, you probably wished many times that that kind of relationship could have been different. Why couldn't there be a prevention program that would help us keep those kinds of relationships from developing? There is!

CRITICAL TIMES

For all of us, there are critical times in our lives when we make choices that either help to set into motion the love-hate relationships that will drain and harass us or help to set in motion the healthy, nurturing kinds of relationships we all long to have.

We really have no choice about the family into which we are born; but when it comes time to start our own family, we are faced with a multitude of choices. How we make those choices will be critical in developing a prevention plan.

Almost everyone begins marriage with idealized expectations. Feelings of "we're going to be different" affect almost all of us. There is nothing wrong with wanting to succeed, but the end of the honeymoon usually marks the beginning of unrealized and unrealizable expectations. To avoid the beginning of a new love-hate relationship, these expectations must be resolved. A good way to work on correcting expectations is to talk about them.

Most couples simply expect their marriage to become what they want it to be—automatically. It will just happen. But dreams that are unexpressed seldom occur. And this is especially true in relationships.

An exercise I often encourage couples to do is to write out a description of how they imagine their marriage will be in five years and to assume that it will be perfect for them. Each person is to write out his or her dream and assume that all problems are resolved. When the dreams are in writing, they share their dreams with each other. Often the dreams are quite similar, with the only difference being the order in which things are written.

After sharing their dreams, the couple work together to come up with one common dream. Then they translate the dream into a statement of goals for their marriage. It becomes a five-year plan that can be broken down into smaller goals and steps.

This way of articulating dreams also will reveal expectations.

As these are brought out into the open, they can be discussed and brought closer into line with reality.

Another critical time is when a man and woman become parents for the first time. All of the priorities and expectations come to a jarring bump with reality. A relationship between two people is easy when compared to the complexities of three people. Add to that the fatigue that accompanies having a newborn infant, and you have the ingredients for confusion and accumulation of hurts and misunderstandings.

These critical times of new beginnings are the times to remember that we have choices. We do not need to give in to the initial hurts. To endure in silence or to hold a grudge will only lay the groundwork for future love-hate relationships. Time must be allowed for adjustments. Time must be taken to talk about feelings, hurts, and expectations.

EMOTIONAL POLARITIES

If you've passed those two critical times in your life, or haven't reached them yet, there is still an important prevention process for you to experience. An important foundational point is to understand the polarities we experience in love-hate relationships.

When I both love and hate someone, I am caught in the back-and-forth tension of emotional polarity. This tendency grows out of a division within us that divides feelings and objects into polar opposites of "either-or." Either the other person is good, or the other person is bad. Either I feel love for this person, or I feel hate. There is no in-between.

In the first chapter, we looked at Sarah's love-hate relationship with her father. When she is with her alcoholic father, he becomes all-bad. She is filled with feelings of anger, hatred, and determination never to see him again. She can see only the bad parts of her dad, and they are so overpowering that she can see nothing else.

When she has been away from him for several days, she begins to forget or excuse his badness. She begins to deny his bad parts and look only at the things she likes about him. Her guilt forces her to bury her anger and hatred, and she ends up going to see him again—only to feel the emotions do a flip-flop to the opposite side. Then she is filled with anger at his alcoholism and lack of feeling for her.

Sarah can't find a comfortable in-between place where she can acknowledge the emotional hurts she experiences with her dad and also see the love she feels for him and the longing for a good relationship with him.

In chapter 2, we saw how this process of splitting begins in infancy, when it is a natural part of our early development. But when we experience emotional splitting as an adult, it leads to nothing but pain and trauma in our lives. For adults, splitting is part of the process of denial. We acknowledge one part of reality, but we are forced to deny the opposite part. It is the same as all-or-nothing thinking, which draws us into a push-pull experience with our emotions. We try to keep people in categories of either all-good, all-loving, all-nice, or all-bad, all-nasty, all-despised. There is no middle ground.

For example, Bill can only see his mom as either all-good or all-bad. Either she is a saint who can do no wrong, or he can't stand the thought of her. If you asked Bill about his mom, the answer would depend on the day you asked. When he is with her, the tension rises quickly as Bill gets into an argument with her and ends up shouting at her on his way out the door. Before he gets home, though, the guilt sets in and Mom is a saint for a while.

An interesting thing takes place with Bill. When he is angry at his mom and they are arguing, he feels good about himself. He is all-good and she is all-bad. But later, when the guilt sets in, Bill switches to being all-bad and Mom becomes all-good again. If you talked with Bill about all of this, he might be able to understand what is happening, but his conversation would be filled with the phrase "Yes, but . . ." He would say things like, "I know my mom drives me crazy, *but* she does the best she can," or "I can't stand to be around her, *but* she is my mom and I owe it to her."

Another example of this occurs when we see our own faults in someone else. It is easy to be critical of the other person and even to "write them off" in our lives. But we can't see the same problem in ourselves. Jesus spoke of this when he said, "Why do you look at the speck of sawdust in your brother's eye and pay no attention to the plank in your own eye?" (Matt. 7:3). We do that because we project our own badness onto the other, splitting it off from ourselves, so we can experience ourselves as being good.

Sometimes the reverse is true. We become overwhelmed with our own badness and believe that everyone else is good. We split off our goodness and project it onto others. We're left with a sense of badness that is all-pervasive: we are all bad.

"BOTH-AND" THINKING

We've looked at how this process of splitting is at the root of our love-hate relationships. The truth is, life is not that way. Life is not either-or. It is both-and.

I remember growing up in a church in which a person was considered nothing more than a worm. Humans were all-bad. And even when we had received salvation, we were still considered worthless.

It wasn't until Francis Schaefer's books came out that we were brought back to a more biblical, balanced view of the nature of man. Yes, it is true: "There is no one righteous, not even one" (Rom. 3:10). But it is also true that man is the crown jewel of all creation. The psalmist affirms that God "made him [man] a little lower than the heavenly beings and crowned him with glory and honor" (Ps. 8:5). Man is *both* good *and* bad.

In practical terms, we struggle with the "both-and" when we are unable to be angry with someone and still care deeply about that person. We can be hurt by someone's behavior and still be willing to care about that person and talk it through with him or her.

Both-and thinking allows us to hold on to opposite points of truth. A common example of this is when four people, on four different corners of an intersection, observe an accident in the middle of that intersection. Each person reports the "truth" about the accident, but all four reports are different. How can they be truthful and yet be different? In this example it is easy to see that the unique perspective of each witness led him or her to report what was seen from a particular vantage point. But no one had a complete view of what took place. They all spoke the truth, but no one was completely accurate.

When I see couples in counseling, one of the "rules" I have for the sessions is that everyone is right. When each tells me how he or she sees the problem, the stories may sound like opposites; but the rule is, "You are both right." Some people are really bothered by that. They operate on the premise that only one person can be right. They are caught up in either-or thinking, and that keeps them locked into their love-hate position.

The complete truth is much bigger than either person can see. No one can fully know everything about any situation. They can't know circumstances for the other person; they can't know motives or feelings experienced by the other person; they can't see the event from the other person's point of view. The complete truth is much bigger than one point of view. It's only when both people can realize this that they can stop the destructive cycle of trying to convince the other and can begin to work on the resolution of the problem. Both-and thinking frees people from the bondage of love-hate relationships and opens the doorway to resolution and forgiveness.

To live in the tension between what appears to be opposite truths requires certain qualities. One must have learned from experience that what appears to be clear isn't really that clear when we hear the other person's point of view. This level of maturity includes an objectivity that surpasses one's own subjectiveness to let the person see there is another side to the issue. This maturity also has with it an attitude that seeks forgiveness, not justification. This attitude of forgiveness will allow the person to seek the healing of the relationship *and* be willing to confront the denial in self or the other. It is a maturity that is able to live "in-between" with a concern for *both* grace *and* truth.

EXPRESSION OF FEELINGS

Not only must we learn to accept the good and the bad in any situation or any person, but we need to learn how to express what we are feeling—both good and bad.

The person who is operating under either-or thinking will automatically assume that any expression of the bad will end the relationship. This is a faulty perception and only serves to encourage the growth of love-hate relationships. We protect ourselves from love-hate relationships by learning how to express negative feelings in a way that leads to positive out-comes. This requires the ability to see the good at the same time we see the bad. The case study in the first chapter described how Joe and Betty must learn to express their hurt and dismay at Daren's behavior *and* still see the good that is in him. This begins in their thoughts, where they must hold on to the good parts of Daren at the same time they deal with the destructive behaviors.

I've worked with parents, especially fathers, who can only see the bad parts of their children. Their only contact with the kids is to criticize or to attempt to change them. When I attempt to bring the good parts of the kid back into focus, the dad sits there and shakes his head. He can't see it. He can't live "in-between." And as it was for Joe and Betty, fathers' relationships with their kids will not improve until they can see both sides at the same time.

SPEAKING THE TRUTH IN LOVE

Paul's urging to the Ephesians to speak "the truth in love" (Eph. 4:15) is an example of expressing both good and bad feelings. Some people read that verse and believe it says, "Speak the truth no matter who it hurts," while others read it as saying, "Speak only in love about parts of the truth." Both of these extremes are examples of either-or thinking. What Paul is calling us to do is an example of both-and thinking. The truth must be conveyed in an attitude of love.

The "truth" implies that I speak about all of what I am feeling—both good and bad. Speaking in love implies that I am able to communicate it so that the outcome is positive. But how do I do that? Here are three suggestions:

• CHOOSE THE RIGHT TIME

This doesn't just mean time as shown on a clock—it goes beyond that. Choosing the right time means that I am ready to talk about both the good and the bad. It means I have worked through my own feelings of hurt and outrage and now can talk to the other person honestly and openly. I can talk about my feelings of hurt and anger without losing my temper or falling into a pattern of blaming. Choosing the right time means I have already started working on my attitude of forgiveness even before I talk to the other person.

• CHOOSE THE RIGHT PLACE

If I am choosing the right time, as described above, it will be easier for me to choose the right place. To talk with this other person, I need a place that will be safe for both of us—a place where we can feel like we are on equal footing. I want to be sensitive to the feelings of the other person so I can maximize the probability that he or she will hear what I need to say.

• CHOOSE TO LISTEN

Most of the time when we need to share what we are feeling, our primary concern is talking, not listening. This is especially true between parent and child. But the fact is, in any type of relational conflict, the key to satisfactory resolution is the ability to listen. We are people who don't take the time to listen. One of the primary things a pastoral counselor or therapist does is listen. I've had people tell me that I am the only one who really hears what they are trying to say. How tragic, but how common! Being able to express my feelings in a healing way requires that I concentrate on listening also.

This means parents, like Joe and Betty, need to listen to what their kids are saying to them. And we need to listen not only to the words but to the feelings behind the words that are so difficult to express. This means we need to listen to the person we both love and hate. And perhaps most of all, it means we need to listen to ourselves. We need to hear that inner voice, prompted by God's Spirit, telling us to pay attention to what is going on. Listening also means we need to hear things about ourselves that need attention. Often the persons we both love and hate are the ones who know us well, and there is some truth in what they want to say to us.

REBUILDING SELF-ESTEEM

Preventing future love-hate relationships means we have to rebuild our image of ourselves. One of the things experienced in a love-hate relationship is the eroding of our sense of self. The development of both-and thinking is a foundation stone in the rebuilding of our self-esteem, for it allows us to see the value and worth of the other person in a balanced, realistic way. This leads us to see ourselves in the same balanced way.

Taking the risk of sharing both our good and bad feelings will be another building block in the rebuilding of our self-esteem. When I can take that risk and experience the openness and genuineness of that kind of relationship, I feel better about myself. And as my good feelings about myself grow, I begin to try new things, and these in turn add to my self-esteem.

Perhaps the most important step in the rebuilding of our self-esteem is the willingness to make amends for the past. People in a recovery program for alcoholism make a fearless moral inventory of themselves. After they have worked through this step and talked with a trustworthy person about what is on their list, the next step is to make amends with those they can—as long as it won't add more hurt. The crux of their recovery is making amends. This is true in any recovery program, including recovery from love-hate relationships.

The reason another person is involved in this part of the process is that it is crucial to know when making amends will be healing and when it could be harmful. When making amends could be harmful, the healing within me must come from being able to talk it through with someone I can trust. This can be a pastor, a counselor, or a wise friend.

As these building blocks to our self-esteem become a part of us, we will find the inner courage that will allow us never to accept failure as final. Setbacks will only be temporary. When we fall, we *will* get up again. We know there will be failures, but knowing that keeps them from being final.

LEARNING TO ACCEPT MYSELF

When Paul writes to the church in Rome, he suggests in the twelfth chapter that the members make a "sane estimate" of themselves. What he means by a "sane estimate" is one that is not too high, which is the less common error, and not too low, which is much more common.

Preventing love-hate relationships means we know ourselves, in terms of both strengths and weaknesses. If you sat down with a pad of paper with two columns, you would probably find it much easier to fill the column of negative qualities about yourself. To develop a balanced picture, you will probably need the help of someone who knows and likes you. When that person suggests you write something in the positive column, do it! Don't argue or minimize the suggestion. Then read the list of positives a number of times until you can actually begin to believe they are true.

People who have struggled with love-hate relationships are often extremely hard on themselves. You need to give yourself permission to make mistakes. In my book *Living with a Perfectionist*, I encourage the perfectionist to purposely make mistakes and then observe what they feel after making those mistakes. Usually they are upset because they have let down their "ideal self." It's true that we only learn from our mistakes, and one of the things we learn is that we can still accept ourselves. Give your real self a break!

PRACTICE, PRACTICE, PRACTICE

If it looks like it will take time, you are correct. A healthy self doesn't occur instantly. It takes practice. If I want to be an excellent tennis player, I don't just pick up a tennis racquet and assume I will beat the pro in my first game. That's absurd. We know that being good at tennis or any other sport requires that we practice, practice, and practice some more. It means we get help from an instructor when we can't figure out what we are doing wrong. And it means that we play tennis whenever we can. Building a healthy you, and building healthy relationships, will take practice and will take time.

Practice also implies discipline. If I need to lose weight, I can't just wish myself thinner. I have to have the discipline to practice consistent changes in my eating patterns. I need to be aware of what a healthy diet is and then discipline myself to eat that way. Building a healthy you, and building healthy relationships, requires discipline, too. We need to be aware of what is happening, and we need to discipline ourselves to work on the changes consistently.

There was a commercial on TV a few years ago. It involved changing the oil filter on your car. At the end of the commercial, the mechanic looked at the camera and said, "You can pay me now, or you can pay me later." The implication is that an oil filter now costs very little compared to the cost of rebuilding your engine later. He has a point—which also applies to building a healthy you and building healthy relationships. The time to begin is *now*. Waiting only makes it more difficult.

TYPES OF LOVE

In preventing love-hate relationships, it is important that we recognize the different ways we can express love. At the bottom of the scale would be *self-centered* love. This is the love that's often found on one side of a love-hate relationship. This type of love is only interested in what it can get. The other person's needs don't even exist. This is the kind of love that a newborn child gives. He or she really doesn't give love but only receives it. The adoring parent interprets smiles and so on as expressions of love, but the infant is only able to receive love at that stage.

Moving up the scale a notch, we find a type of love that is always *making a deal*. It's the kind of love that responds to and tests limits. It is the type of love that says, "I will love you because I don't want to be punished," or "I'll be a good girl or boy because I know that if I'm not, you'll get mad at me." It is a love that is expressed only out of the fear of the consequences of not expressing it. In chapter 1, Sandra's behavior toward her ex-husband is an example of this type of love.

The next type of love on the scale is the "What's in it for me?" type of love. This is the kind of love Dan experienced in his love-hate relationship with his boss. He was caught in the bind because it gave him pleasure in many ways. It made him look good to his coworkers, who gladly would have traded places with him if they could. This kind of love feels very much like self-centered love, but it is different in that it is expressed in ways that are more acceptable to those watching.

This is the kind of love that keeps a daughter in a trap of caring for an aging, belligerent parent because she is afraid of what others would think if she did anything different. It's the kind of love that binds us with guilt.

Moving up another notch, we come to the type of love that is the *right thing to do*. This is a more mature type of love that recognizes commitments and loyalties at its base. This is the type of love that can often bloom into a beautiful, lasting relationship, filled with caring. It is the kind of love we want to experience, but there is one weakness. Sometimes this kind of love is pulled in several directions, and then there are no clear rules for how to act. Sometimes, also, the hurts can grow over the years, and this type of love will finally give up. But aside from these tests, this type of love is mature and usually doesn't lead us into love-hate relationships.

At the top of the scale is the type of love that loves *even when it hurts*. This love is what the Bible refers to as *agape* love. Here, love is a virtue. Love goes on regardless of circumstances, always willing to forgive and sacrifice for the other. But this type of love also is able to confront hurts and call the other person to accountability. It is not a passive love that turns us into doormats; it is an active love that is always reaching out to the other, speaking the truth in love.

As you look at these five types of love, you can see that the first three are the types of love that draw us into love-hate relationships. These relationships develop when one of those types is either the way we love or the way the other loves us.

Recognizing the immature levels of love and knowing their characteristics can help us protect ourselves from future love-hate relationships.

WHAT TO DO IN THE FUTURE

In summary, what can you do in the future to protect yourself from the bind of a love-hate relationship? Here are three steps:

• RECOGNIZE IT

Be aware. Recognize the potential for a love-hate conflict early in the relationship. Be aware of relationships in which you are not able to express comfortably what you feel. Recognize situations in which you are forced to split your emotions into good and bad categories. Be alert to people who want to be with you but are only able to express immature types of love. These, and other points covered in the book, are signals you need to pay attention to so you can avoid being drawn into an unhealthy situation.

• RESPOND TO THE PROCESS

When we have struggled to break free from past love-hate relationships, we may be very wary of anything that feels the same. If we recognize the potential for a love-hate relationship, we'll often feel like running. Before you run, though, respond to the process of what is happening, not to the person. For example, if we assume that Sandra, whom we met in the first chapter, is able to break out of the unhealthy relationship with her ex-husband, her reaction would be to run when she meets anyone else who even reminds her of him. But as she becomes healthier, she may find herself in a relationship with a man who suddenly does something that reminds her of her ex-husband. It is important at that point that she respond to what is happening, not to the other person.

Sandra needs to communicate what she is feeling, including the fears and old hurts that have crowded into her awareness. If she says something like, "I'm really feeling afraid right now. What just happened brought back to me a lot of old hurts. We need to talk about it." Notice, she didn't accuse the other person of doing what her ex did; nor is she blaming him. She is confronting what is happening, not the other person.

• REFUSE TO PLAY THE GAME

If, when Sandra confronts the behavior, the other person continues to act in a way that pushes her into the bind that will lead to a new love-hate relationship, Sandra needs to withdraw from the game. This may mean that she leaves the situation temporarily. It might mean that she will break off the relationship if she is unable to clear things up. Whatever she does, she cannot get into a victim's role again, and she cannot excuse the other person's behavior if it continues.

These three steps recognize that prevention of love-hate relationships rests solely with me. I am responsible for the decision I make. The healthier I am, the healthier my decisions will be. No one develops a healthy relationship if one person is not healthy. And no one can become healthy without developing healthy relationships.

Chapter Eight

FORGIVING PARENTS . . .
FORGIVING CHILDREN . . .
FORGIVING PARENTS . . .

CHILDREN HAVE NEEDS—MANY NEEDS. THERE'S NOTHING new about that. Everyone knows that children are needy little people. It is also common knowledge that there are parents who meet those needs and parents who do not. Some parents care enough to put forth the best effort possible to meet the needs of their children, and some parents are just too sick, selfish, or lazy to care. Their first decision to have children was a mistake, followed by repeated mistakes of neglect, irresponsibility, and other forms of emotional and physical abuse. The love-hate relationship was in place before birth, and it blossomed after birth.

NEEDY CHILDREN AND NASTY PARENTS

The behaviors of these loving-hating parents, the abuse, do not go unnoticed by their children. The children learn the abusive patterns and repeat them with their own children. The destruction is repeated over and over, causing the sins of the fathers (and mothers) to be passed down, generation after generation. The love and hate from parent to child and child to parent powerfully lock each new generation into the sickness of the previous generation. But the chain can be broken. The cycle can be stopped. When parents decide to make a difference in the lives of their children, when parents decide to set their children free to become all that God allows—then the locks are unlatched and the abuse of one generation stops with that generation.

PARENTS WHO PROVIDE

Parents who care enough to free their children from an inheritance of emotional turmoil can be very happy with the results. Few things are more satisfying than watching free children achieve their dreams. The possibilities are limitless. Someone will become the parent of the inventor of ice cream that will not melt. Someone may be the parent of a parent of the first leader of a nation on another planet. Someone's child will make great strides in solving world hunger.

With children unrestricted by emotional garbage from the early years, the possibilities are unfathomable. But great children who do great things are not an accident. They are taught by their parents. And they are taught by example.

Children need to be taught many things. There are very special principles and concepts God wants parents to teach their children. Teaching how to keep a commitment and how to make and uphold vows are God's precepts that need to be instilled in children by example. Prayer, sacrifice, giving, and worship are godly talents that too few parents teach.

I saw a wonderful example of a son who knew how to show

his love to his father. I parked at Houston Hobby Airport, dropping off my friend Jim Burns, who was flying home. Just before he opened the door to get out, we both were stopped by the scene we saw through the rear window of the car in front of us. There we observed a young man, about sixteen years old, reach across the seat and clutch his father, hugging him tightly, his eyes squinting from the sincere emotion of the moment. Jim and I were deeply moved by the intensity of the expression. There was no bitterness, anger, or hatred within the embrace. Pure love, taught by a father and given back by a son. To love is an art that must be practiced alongside real-life models. Parents make the best models for teaching how to love.

LOVE FORGIVES

Love has many components and dimensions. It is not all emotion; it is in part great effort. One dimension that requires great effort is the act of forgiveness. Love, in its most liberating form, forgives. Forgiveness is difficult and complicated. It has its best chance to present itself when one has learned it from a parent over years of observation. If children are to be forgiving, their parents must teach the art of forgiveness.

Scripture has a beautiful example of two boys who were taught to forgive through the example of a father. In Luke 15:11, there begins the story of the prodigal son. The story could be relabeled "the forgiving father." This story is full of love-hate tension between father and son, son and father, brother and brother. In the story told by Jesus, the youngest brother asked for his share of the inheritance and the father divided his property between the two sons. The younger brother took all that was his and set off for a distant country. There he squandered his wealth in wild living. Once all of the money was gone, a famine struck the land. In his desperation he hired himself out to a citizen who sent him to the fields to feed pigs. He was so hungry he wanted to eat the food the pigs were devouring. But no one gave him anything, not even pig food.

This was not an entirely stupid son. It did not take him long to come to his senses and realize that back home at his father's place, the people who worked for his father had food to spare. He was starving while Dad's servants ate well. So he planned a speech to deliver to his father, left the pigs, and went home. But long before he reached his father, his father saw him coming and was so full of compassion that he ran to him and hugged and kissed him.

The young son confessed that he had sinned and was not worthy to be called "Son." But the father did not respond in the way the boy had expected. He told his servants to bring the best robe and put it on the boy and to bring a ring for his finger and sandals for his feet. He told them to kill the fattened calf and prepare a feast and a celebration. He told them that his son had been dead but was now alive. He said that the boy had been lost but now was found. And they began to celebrate. The father showed his young son that he had forgiven him totally, fully, with no "I told you so's."

RESENTFUL SON, REPENTANT SON

But the young boy's older brother was not so gracious. When he came out of the fields and heard music and dancing from the celebration, he asked a servant what was going on. The servant told him about the celebration for his younger brother. This made the older brother furious, and he refused to go in the house. When his father realized that the boy was outside, he went out to him and pleaded for him to understand. But the boy could only express his disgust and envy. He told his father that for years he had obediently worked for him. He complained that his father had never even provided so much as a goat for a barbecue with his friends. He went on to remind his father that his brother had squandered away his share of the family property with such activities as cavorting with prostitutes, yet when he came home, there was a celebration, and the fattened calf was killed for him.

The father tried to explain his motives behind his forgiving, loving treatment of the younger son. He told the older boy that he had always been with him and thus the older boy was entitled to everything the father had. It was all his. He told him that there had to be a celebration with plenty of gladness. He repeated that his younger son had been dead and was alive again, that he had been lost but now was found.

In this powerful story, a father taught two sons how to forgive by forgiving. His example of forgiveness could not have been more powerful for either son, the repentant one or the resentful one. Both learned a lesson that surely was long remembered by both. That father certainly must have been tempted to utter, "I knew it would come to this," or to remark, "Maybe you will listen to me now." But instead he offered forgiveness as a model of the forgiveness that Christ provided for all of us. We do not deserve it, yet all of us are worthy of it. That was the message that a forgiving father gave to two brothers, one

FORGIVING PARENTS . . . FORGIVING CHILDREN . . .   123

repentant and one resentful. I believe that both brothers noticed and neither forgot.

JUNIOR HIGH FORGIVENESS

My wife and I work with a group of junior high school students. In an exercise one Sunday, I asked them to write out why they loved their father so much. One wrote the following: "Because he always forgives me. A lot of times he's understanding, like the time I got suspended. He understood where I was coming from. He cares what I do." When parents forgive their children, they notice. It is one lesson that lasts a lifetime.

A friend of mine, John Snyder, has a son who is nine years old and is an excellent athlete, a premier pitcher. He just happens to play for the worst Little League team in baseball history. John's son Jake was the best thing the team had going for it. Jake saved games and won games for his squad until one day. On that day he pitched so badly that he single-handedly lost the game. The team had never lost because of him before. He did not even need the rest of his crummy teammates to pitch in with their errors, strikeouts, and players left on base. He was responsible for the loss. After the game, he told his father that his baseball career was over. He wanted to hang up his glove and never return to the mound. He was finished.

John did not know whether it was better to let Jake walk away or to encourage him to play again. Of one thing he was sure: Jake did not need a scolding from him. Unlike other Little League parents, John did not yell, spit, scold, or deride his son either in public or in private. Instead, he told him of all the strikeouts Babe Ruth had had. He told Jake of his belief that the team needed him. And as a result, Jake suited up again, returned to the mound, pitched, and won. A budding baseball career was saved.

Jake, like most little boys, did not present what I believe was the real issue, the unspoken question. Jake's dramatic reaction and avowal not to return to the mound was his "little boy" way of discovering something very important to him. It was his way of discovering whether or not he would be forgiven by his father for the loss. And the wonderful way John talked with his son proved to his star baseball player that he was forgiven. A potential baseball career was saved, but more important, so was a little boy's heart.

Did you ever stop and think back on the times when your child's extreme behavior might have been an attempt to find reassurance in forgiveness from a parent? Every day in thousands of ways, children are asking parents, "Do you forgive me?" Dashed expectations often lead parents to consciously or unconsciously give the message, "You are not forgiven," or "I'm not going to forget this one." But when a parent responds with a resounding act of unconditional love by showing forgiveness, the children notice.

MODERN PRODIGALS

I noticed when my parents started showing their forgiveness of me. It did not mean they approved of what I did or prevent them from punishing me. But it did allow me to start over with a clean slate, a new beginning. The first major incident came when I was in junior high school and a new driver.

Some of my friends and I maliciously harassed a geography teacher by running our cars through her yard. One of the boys was caught, and when pressured he revealed all of the others who had been involved in the evil conspiracy. It was not a happy time for me, having to face my father with my wrongs in order to be admitted back into school.

My father took me over to the lady's house and had me confess to her and ask for her forgiveness. No other guilty student had to do that. My father wanted me to feel the full weight of the consequences of my behavior. But when the ordeal was over, he assured me that he had forgiven me for what I had done and for the embarrassment I had caused him and the rest of the family.

The second time my parents showed their forgiveness also involved a driving problem. My friends and I calculated that the wheels of our Pontiac Catalina were the same width as the railroad tracks. We determined that with careful skill we could drive the car between two streets that intersected the tracks. I did quite well for a while, but on the first curve I curved too much. The car slid from the tracks and slammed down onto the cross ties, the under-frame snagged on the tracks. By the time the car had been removed from the tracks, it was in need of repair. My father also determined that my rear end was in need of repair, and he delivered the appropriate punishment swiftly and effectively. But he forgave me, as did my mother. They let me drive again.

The third time that they reassured me with their forgiveness was a much more serious matter. You see, my father had three very prodigal sons. We made the one in the Bible look like a rookie. I was the first prodigal son to come back home. It was after I had gone off to a Christian college that cost much more than the state university that my brothers attended. I justified the expense to them by emphasizing the Bible teaching I would receive there. But reading the Bible was not how I spent my time. I was promiscuous and sexually active. Eventually a girl I dated became pregnant by me. We consulted no one, and in our isolation, we decided to have an abortion. I helped pay for the abortion of my child.

It is not my intent to make people who have had abortions feel guilty, but I felt that I had been responsible for the death of a child. I also knew that the beautiful young girl would not feel so beautiful anymore. I felt that I had terminated one life and greatly distorted another. The pangs of guilt clawed at my soul, and my emotions of grief overwhelmed me. I had to discuss it with someone. I chose my parents as the ones to help me break out of the silence that was causing me to experience temporary insanity. I went to them because I knew that they would forgive me and reassure me. They did, and my wounds, rather than become infected, began to heal.

My oldest brother was the second prodigal son to come back home. I am not going to confess his sins for him. He had his own problems and worked through them. Now he is a deacon in a Baptist church. My parents' forgiveness and understanding were key to his rededication of his life to God's will.

The third prodigal son who came home was my middle brother, Jerry. He was a talented, brilliant man whom I looked up to for most of my life. When he came back home as a prodigal son, he came back as a repentant homosexual, dying of AIDS. His welcome home was not like the return of the prodigal son in the Bible. My father did not run to him; he drove to a hospital to hear his confession. There were no sandals for his feet; he was not going anywhere. There was no robe, only a hospital gown. There was no ring, just an IV needle in his hand. There was no fattened calf, just the IV solution to help sustain his life. And there was no feast, because there was no appetite. But there was a celebration that the prodigal son had come home, repentant and prepared to enter heaven. It was the ultimate resolution of the love-hate relationship my parents had maintained with Jerry since learning about his homosexual lifestyle.

And then there was another celebration. Jerry died June 13, 1988, and on the following Wednesday, there was a wonderful celebration of what Jerry had done and what God had done through Jerry to bring triumph from the tragedy. Jerry, with my parents' permission, told his story in the book *How Will I Tell My Mother?* As a result, stacks of letters and hours of phone calls attested to the fact that God had used Jerry's struggle to prevent others from having to repeat it. Romans 8:28 was played out in my brother's life because Jerry knew that he could go to my parents and they would forgive him. He knew that even though he had become every parent's nightmare, my parents would not reject him; they would provide the forgiveness and assurance he needed. If he had not known that their response would be forgiveness, he would have died a lonely, painfully secretive death. His life would have counted for very little. But because of forgiving parents, his life and death have helped others to live beyond the trap of homosexuality and find victory as they come out of their struggle.

In his book, written shortly before his death, Jerry wrote the following:

The Bible says God never sends us a problem we cannot handle with His power. It also says He will provide comfort. In both cases, the Scriptures have held true for me. I have grown close to a sweet and loving Jesus and understand that sickness and disease do not come from Him. Our God is there to help us fight the evil forces. I have peace and comfort like I have never felt before, even though I know AIDS continues to ravage my immune system. I pray each night for all who have been afflicted. I pray that God will comfort all of us and our families. God is a good God and a perfect God, and a forgiving God.

For me, during these difficult times of struggle, as each day grows darker, a new dawn draws closer. That closeness to the God I love gives me a superhuman peace and sensitivity that keeps me filled with hope for a new and better day.

> Sing, O heavens!
> Be joyful, O earth!
> And break out in singing, O mountains!
> For the LORD has comforted His people,
> And will have mercy on His afflicted.
>
> ISAIAH 49:13 (NKJV)

Those are the words of a struggler, but a forgiven struggler. Jerry was unencumbered with the guilt of condemnation from the past deeds that had led to his untimely death. There was no bitterness in his thoughts, no hatred toward a God who would allow a disease like AIDS, no hatred toward his parents or even himself. The love-hate paradox had been replaced by a deep acceptance and love.

Because of parents who pointed him toward God's forgiveness, Jerry died feeling forgiven. He had noticed the lessons of forgiveness that my parents had set before him. He said in his final days, "God has forgiven me; nature has not." He said that he had fought a battle with Satan and that God had won. I thank God for parents who led their son to the forgiveness found in Jesus Christ.

God taught us to forgive others by doing it Himself. My father taught my brothers and me to forgive by doing it himself, over and over and over again. Because of his example, I feel forgiven even though I have committed some of the most destructive sins possible. Because of Christ's sacrifice and my parents' example that pointed me toward Christ's forgiveness, I am free from a past of which I could never be proud.

Parents often find themselves with children who have pasts of which they are ashamed. Ever since Adam and Eve had Cain and Abel, parents have had problems with their children. They are not always going to meet the expectations set before them. They will embarrass, rebel, stray, hurt, and disappoint. They will let their parents down repeatedly. And when they do, God wants parents to forgive those children, to show them how to forgive by forgiving, and then forgiving again. For all things big and small, God wants parents to teach their children how to forgive by forgiving.

FAMILIES UNABLE TO FORGIVE

Many people did not have parents who taught them how to forgive. They hurt deeply because they did not have "Ozzie and Harriet" or "the Cleavers" as parents. Their fathers didn't "know best." Their fathers and mothers did not care or, as mentioned at the beginning of the chapter, were too sick or lazy to teach what God wanted taught.

There are a lot of sick parents out there. With over one-third of all females and an eighth of all males being sexually molested before they graduate from high school, it is obvious there are too many "less-than-model" parents. The rampant prevalence of alcoholism has forced at least one-third of all children to be raised in the home of an addict. Divorce is a plague in this century that has caused grown children to live with unresolved insecurities from a broken childhood and a broken marriage.

Children are not always raised in homes where a healthy environment leads to stable development. Some are raised in homes where God's teachings are irrelevant. Instead of learning godly behaviors, they learn to get drunk, to yell, and to scream. The parents, by example, teach the children how to break commitments and how to abandon those who depend on them. Some are taught to worship money or to assault sexually. Many learn early the lesson of how to disappoint. Because of these sorry lessons, the children hate their parents. The venom of that hatred has been poisoning them all of their lives. They have formed a bitter core that only one powerful act can dissolve. It is the act of forgiveness.

THE PRODIGAL REVISITED

Let's go back to the story of the prodigal son. Imagine tuning in to the lives of the father and two sons ten or fifteen years after the return of the lost son. Imagine a scene in which a restless father approaches his two boys to tell them he has sold the farm and is leaving them to fend for themselves. Left stranded without a form of employment, the boys are forced to find jobs to keep themselves from starving. You can imagine the reaction of two boys who are used to working in the family business. Having worked on the farm all of their lives, they ill prepared for the challenge of making it on their own. They are forced from a life of owning servants into servanthood themselves, all because their father became greedy and selfish and went on his own way.

Imagine the boys working one day, cleaning out some horse stalls, when their father appears to ask for their forgiveness. The one son, the prodigal son, hugs his father and takes the ring off his own finger and gives it to his father. He finds the robe given to him on his own return and places it on his father's shoulder. He calls for his brother to join him in celebrating the return of his father. But the resentful brother cannot rejoice. In his self-consuming anger he approaches his father and begins to preach:

"You deserted us when we needed you the most. You were not there at our lowest times. How can you expect to walk back into my life as if nothing has happened, as if you are entitled to be forgiven? I will never forgive you for what you have done to me. I hate you!"

In this imaginary extension of Christ's parable, it is not hard to imagine which son will grow up and live a long and happy life. It is easy to see which son will probably die a bitter death. The question of the moment is, which of us has gone the way of a bitter son or a bitter daughter? Which of us is continuing to poison him- or herself with bitter venom of hatred toward a parent? Who is unwilling to forgive?

EXCEPTION OR EXAMPLE

As I discussed this concept with a friend of mine, it became obvious that she maintained a horrible grudge toward her neglectful father. She told me that she did not want to forgive him. And she was not interested in hearing the benefits of forgiveness. There are numerous reasons why some people refuse to forgive their parents. They believe that the offense was too great to warrant forgiveness. They believe it was the worst thing that could possibly have been done. Or they do not forgive because they do not believe their parents are sorry for what they did. At least if they are sorry, they never said so. Nor did they ever ask for forgiveness; so they are not going to get it at least until a request is made. Others withhold forgiveness because there were repeated transgressions that may be repeated again. And others do not forgive because they believe their parents deserve to be punished for the hurts of their past.

The central theme in all of these reasons is that the unforgiving children who hold on to their hate believe that they are the exception to God's command to forgive. They somehow believe that even God in heaven would not expect forgiveness in their circumstances. But every time we believe we are the exception, God wants us to be the example to the rest of the world. God wants us to stand up before those who do not deserve forgiveness and gladly hand it over to them. The greater the hurt, the greater the example to the rest of the world. God wants to take exceptional abuse and turn the forgiveness of that abuse into the model of Christ's forgiveness that is available to all who believe in Him.

A LIFESTYLE OF FORGIVENESS

Forgiveness is not easy. It does not mean that inappropriate behavior is to be tolerated. It is not intended to enable the abuse to be continued. It does not excuse the destructive nature of a person. And again, it is not easy. But forgiveness is trying to see life from the vantage point of the parent. It is understanding that the abusiveness was probably learned from the parent's own abusive parents. It is seeing the parent as inadequate, imperfect, and in need of forgiveness. It is seeing him or her as equally worthy of Christ's sacrifice. It is accepting that in life there are no perfect saints, no pure, sinless creatures. Forgiveness is accepting that a parent's faults do not make you faultless. It is stepping off a self-righteous soap box and meeting a parent, even a bad one, where he or she needs to be met. Forgiveness allows God to avenge the wrongs and heal the hurts.

After I spoke on this one Sunday, a man came up to me afterward and said that he had finally forgiven his father after more than thirty years. When he was four years old, a large station wagon came to pick up his mother to take her on a trip. His father did not tell him that it was an ambulance. He didn't let him know that his mother was dying from pneumonia. And she died without his saying good-bye to her. The bitterness and anger at his father's insensitivity grew over the years, distorting his personality and straining his emotions. After years of pain and struggle, he finally took the advice of a minister and forgave his father, openly and to his face. He told his father he forgave him and opened the channels of communication between them. For the first time the man experienced hope for his future. He drained the hate from his lifetime of love-hate with his father. Anyone can.

I heard some good advice from a preacher down in the British Virgin Islands. My wife and I were staying on the island of Tortolla. It had not been a pleasant experience. We had never been to a place where we felt so much anger from the people. And it seemed that all they were interested in was ripping us off. I decided to attend church on Sunday and chose the Caine Garden Bay Baptist Church. The first song that was sung was entitled "It's an Unfriendly World out There." I could not have agreed more but was astounded that they even sing about the unfriendliness of the island. It was an uneasy service for me. The preacher began by exhorting, "Dwelling on the past will destroy you. . . . If it was terrible in the past, you must learn from it and never repeat it . . . Some black people have never forgotten that white man held him slave."

I grew even more uneasy until he said the profound truth of the morning. He proclaimed, "You cannot let the abuse of the past breed further abuse." I inwardly said amen with a big sigh of relief. The potency of that statement may be missed by the casual reader. Abuse must not be allowed to breed further abuse. When people refuse to forgive the abuse from parents, that abuse breeds further abuse in the next generation. That is why such a large percentage of people on death row were abused as children. It is the power of forgiveness that causes a miscarriage of the birth of abuse in the next generation.

Morgan Cryar sings the song "Break the Chain."* It is based
on Deuteronomy 5:9–10.

Suzy's daddy just nags and shouts
She yells back, then they have it out
She wants to run away and get married real bad
But her boyfriend Joe is just like Dad.
Better break the chain

Billy is another kid right across town
His dad left his mom 'cause she held him down
To think about his father just drives him mad
But he uses his girlfriends just like Dad.

Break the chain, break the chain
Cut the cord, end the curse, stop the reign
Break the chain, break the chain
The family sin will do you in, so break the chain

Little Jan was a battered child
She used to hide out while her mama went wild
Will she raise the seed that her mama has sown?
What's she gonna do with kids of her own?
Better break the chain

I could tell Reggie was a preacher's kid
By the fire in his eyes and the things he did
He never heard his father say "I love you"

*"Break the Chain," words by Morgan Cryar, music by Ty Tabor. Copyright ©
1986 by Ariose Music. All rights reserved. Used by permission.

When Reggie has a son tell me what's he gonna do?
He better break the chain . . .

Sometimes sin is just a family tradition
But it'll burn the family tree to the ground
Nobody wants to inherit the flames
You sure don't want to pass 'em down
Break the chain

You can burn the family tree of abuse in the flames of
complete and total forgiveness.

Within the heart of a father or mother is found the image of
God. That image often remains through adulthood. Forgiving
a parent can allow God to be known in a whole new way. But
the complete knowledge of God can be locked away behind a
door of resentment. The key of forgiveness can open that door
and reveal a wonderful, loving, and forgiving God. Today is a
great day to stop the tradition of love-hate and unlock the door
by forgiving a parent.

F. Scott Fitzgerald wrote, "There are no second acts in
American lives." I do not believe that he understood what
Christianity, the power of Christ, and forgiveness are about.
There can be a glorious second act for children and parents
alike. It can begin with the first scene having two characters:
a parent and a child. And in that first scene of the second act,
a child offers forgiveness and a parent accepts. And for the
first time in a long while, they experience love, acceptance,
and forgiveness.

If you were abused when you were young, you must refuse
to let a low blow from your past continue to hurt you. The

pain will stop when forgiveness starts. It all works together to resolve the love-hate relationships of life. God wants parents to teach their children how to forgive, because often children need to know how to forgive their parents. When they do, the bonds of a love-hate relationship are loosened by God Himself.

Chapter Nine

CONCLUSION:
YOU HAVE A DECISION TO MAKE

FOR THOSE WHO HAVE BEEN BRUTALLY VICTIMIZED, IT IS A very tough realization, but an essential concept to be accepted, that there are no victims. At least there are no permanent victims. Sexual abuse as a child does not have to make one weak or deranged thirty years later. A divorce does not have to turn someone into a social outcast for life. In other words, whatever the trauma, external in nature or self-inflicted, it is the responsibility—the mandate—of the traumatized ones to pick themselves up or get help to get up so that they cannot just move on but become stronger for having gone through the trauma.

THERE ARE NO VICTIMS . . .

Often we see people who are involved in one crisis after another. At times this is a result of totally uncontrollable factors. But frequently crises number two, three, four, and five are all a result of crisis number one. This can be the result of a person moving into a victim role and never fighting to change and come out of that role.

Thus, the death of a family member leads to a divorce, and then soon after there is a job loss. Victim, to victim, to victim. The role gets set, and the pattern is repeated time and time again. Looking at the situation, you wonder how things could be so dreadfully terrible for one person. In reality, it could not be so dreadful unless the person began to allow the tragedies to happen. The "victim," caught up in the role, becomes trapped in the negative behaviors that lead from problem to problem. So, in reality, there are no victims, but . . .

. . . THERE ARE POOR DECISION MAKERS

Poor decision makers are not mentally ill, although the results of their poor decisions often look like the work of an insane person. The things they do would seem to drive most people crazy. But their fault is not in the emotional makeup of their minds but in the thinking areas. They decide to marry the most incompatible person. They decide to take a job that is too difficult, resulting in tremendous frustration and eventual firing. They decide to raise their children "by the seat of their pants" rather than reading some helpful books on child rearing. They decide to react to their parent's every complaint or hurting statement, intensifying the conflict rather than resolving it. In each new challenge the "victim" makes a poor decision that produces greater trauma and pain. Life becomes unbearable, not because of the nature of life, but because life's difficulties are magnified into major disasters.

Each poor decision maker, after repeated disasters, learns to obtain some benefits from his or her role as a martyr, thriving on the pity that comes pouring in after each new crisis. They are able to say to themselves that "under the circumstances" just getting by or coping is an accomplishment. These martyrs feel good when others notice how bad their lives have become. They end up feeling morally superior to others who have not endured a similar plight. And all of these secondary gains from martyrdom are difficult to break off. They feed each new crisis and set up the person for the next one. Often, were it not for the pity and condolences, the person believes there would be no attention, no reinforcement, and no one to care.

The martyr becomes trapped because of the false security in the martyr role. This security comes from the predictability of the reaction of others to each new crisis. Unconsciously the martyr makes the poor decision, knowing if things work out, that would be fine. But if they do not work out, then it will be another source of obtaining the denied attention. This trap is totally self-inflicted. It is baited by a sick ego that seeks gratification in a twisted way. The twist is in the poor decision and the lack of effort that goes into the decision-making process.

The worst, most detrimental decision is the decision not to change. Magic, a Prince Charming, or a fairy godmother will not rectify the situation with no effort on the part of the struggler. It takes a decision to change, a tough decision that has will and persistence behind it. The martyr must transform into an adventurer who is not afraid to try life from a different angle, to see it from a different perspective. Instead, the poor decision maker makes the poor decision to stay the same, repeat the past, and suffer the consequences of a life made unfair at his or her own hands. When poor decision makers decide that enough time has been wasted and that it is time to make a change, there is hope for a new life. But most poor decision makers continue in the same pattern, producing the same results of despair and hopelessness.

. . . THERE ARE LAZY PEOPLE, LAZINESS BEING JUST ANOTHER POOR DECISION

You may have been called lazy all of your life. By now you believe that laziness is central to your being. But there are no genes that pass on a biological predisposition to laziness.

Laziness is neither genetic nor permanent. It is a way of life produced one decision at a time. The lazy lifestyle is the culmination of repeated decisions to procrastinate, decisions not to show up, and decisions to exert as little effort as possible. At any point the lazy person can change, but instead he or she remains lazy and stays in the rut of being a victim.

Laziness becomes an expression of helplessness. At times the person believes that people do not see laziness; they see hurting and helplessness. If others see this helplessness, perhaps they will jump in and do what they can to help. Someone must be there to fix everything. Someone must take charge, patch up and clean up after the damage from being lazy. This expression of helplessness is a means to attract those who prey on people caught in the trap of being a victim. Because of laziness, the individual walks out of one relationship and back into another one that is just as sick or sicker than the previous one.

Laziness allows that person to avoid many of the realities of life. Life is full of mundane chores. No one enjoys waiting in line for a driver's license or paying a traffic fine, but the lazy person just decides not to do these things. A decision is made to forget or erase anything that might jog the memory. Consequences of the irresponsible behavior are ignored. So the mundane things become minor crises that inflict more pain on the already existing circumstances. The lazy person, sitting back as a victim, wants, even prays for someone to come along and fix all of these disasters. He or she is waiting for someone to take care of the mundane things, the painful things, the simple things that would require a small amount of effort and some good decisions to fix.

Lazy people also want to avoid other realities of life. The need for growth and development is ignored. So you see these people at age forty or fifty, just as inadequate or immature as they were at age twenty or thirty. They avoid the need to be responsible and the need to do things that lead to maturity. They refuse to delay gratification, to sacrifice, and to do the things that are painful now that produce pleasure later. In ignoring these realities of life or refusing to act on them, they discard the hopeful reality that with effort they can become free. They can work, step by step, to walk out of the rut and into a free and open world where there do not have to be any victims. There are no victims, really. But there are lazy people who seem to be some of the poorest decision makers of all.

. . . THERE ARE ANXIOUS AND FEARFUL PEOPLE

As a by-product of mistrust, there are those who are overwhelmed by fear and anxiety. They believed that someone would always be there, come through, take care of everything—and it did not happen. Or perhaps someone who was trusted turned against them, betrayed them, hurt them, and introduced them to a cruel world where anyone is capable of anything bad and painful. So these people live in a constant state of fear that someone else is going to hurt them. They worry about that a lot. In fact, they worry about it so much, and about everything else, that they become paralyzed. They stop making decisions and stop exerting effort. They find themselves being led around by another person, continually worrying that he or she will stop leading. Life without worry is an unthinkable concept for the anxious. And the way these people hand over the controls of life to others is great cause for worry.

Worry becomes a god for the person acting out a victim role. There develops a hidden belief that worry has power in it, that enough worry really could influence the future. Worry replaces action so that many fears and anxieties prove to be true because the person is paralyzed by the worry and fear. Inaction feeds the worry, and the results of inaction feed the fears so that once again the victim has a perfect self-set trap. These anxious people must do a couple of things. They must forget the untrustworthy people in the past and become trustworthy people in the present. When they resolve the mistrust of the past, they remove the paralyzing effects of the hurt from that past interaction with an untrustworthy person. Then they can make the decision to act in a trustworthy manner, reinforcing the fact that people can be trusted. The more trustworthy they become, the better able they are to trust others and move toward the future without fear. But it takes a decision to do that. It requires a decision to act in uncomfortable ways now to produce a more comfortable life later.

There are people who make decisions that are always poor, producing poor results. There are people who are lazy, who procrastinate in doing what must be done to take charge and refuse to be victimized. And there are people who are riddled with fear and anxiety, worrying about thousands of things that cannot be changed and doing nothing about things that can be changed. These people are not victims. They are not helpless cripples who must flail in their weaknesses for life. No, these are people trapped in a role that they can work out of, freeing themselves from future love-hate relationships. But to change requires decisions and the determination to make those decisions good ones.

. . . THERE ARE THOSE WHO CHOOSE TO REMAIN IN DENIAL

The unwilling people who dig in their heels and refuse to grow find refuge in denial. It alone allows them to remain in their emotional retardation, crippled by their refusal to see reality as it is and to act upon that part of reality that can be changed. Instead of changing themselves and making more of what they have, they latch on to someone else to compensate. This defective grafting allows for existence only and precludes growth and change. Once trapped by the defective grafting, they initially believe that everything will be taken care of, that there is no need to grow, no need to make any effort.

But soon the true colors of the relationship begin to surface and the love-hate pattern becomes set. Rather than acting on the new revelation, these people cram each awareness back down into the denial that becomes a perpetual refuge.

Accompanying the denial is the fear of finding themselves, of coming to know who they really are. In this fear they come to believe the lies that are supported by denial:

"I can't change."

"I must stay in the same situation."

"I do not deserve anything."

"I am worthless."

In accepting the lies, victimized persons place themselves in the control of others. Each day they react to others and are controlled by others. They have sold out to themselves by accepting the lies that reduce them to a miserable existence, dependent on others for their misery. All they would have to do is face the fear of discovering the reality of who they are and accept that reality as the fiber on which to weave their own goals and accomplishments.

In life there are no victims. You become a victim for a short while, but to remain in that state requires some intricate work on unhealthy action and attitudes. It is never too late to move out of that role. It is always time to stop being a victim.

STRUGGLING IN THE GRAY AREAS

There are many who want this to be a black-and-white world where everything is distinctively defined and placed in its proper category. They want to live where good and bad are extremes, where nothing exists in between. They want the clear distinction between acceptable and unacceptable to free them from tough decisions. In a black-and-white world, it is either misery or joy, no room for middle ground. But this is not a black-and-white world. It is not all good or all bad. And at times the fine line between good and bad is so hard to see that it requires strong judgment to determine which is which.

In reality, many people live in a gray world. They do not know extreme joy at any point in their lives. Without extreme highs of wonderful miracles taking place, they may seek out misery to break the monotony of their gray world. But that is not necessary. People can find peace in a gray world. They can resolve their love-hate relationships, reduce their misery, and be at peace with themselves and God. They can find that it is OK to be gray, to live gray, without a black-and-white, easily defined world.

Life is a constant struggle of living in the gray areas. You must struggle not to latch on to the quick highs of drugs, illicit sex, and other vices that momentarily pull you out of the gray. You must struggle to avoid falling prey to the evil in others who would make you their victim if they could. You must stay in the gray if you want to find peace. The dogmatic drivers will try to drive you out of the gray areas that can be peaceful, but you must make the decision to hold on to your gray world and not get trapped in someone else's make-believe black or white. In their black and white will grow the roots of love-hate—roots that you do not have time to let grow or even exist. Life is too short.

FROM VICTIM TO VICTOR

Anyone can do it. In love-hate situations you may have found that you are the loser every time. But there does not have to be a next time. Today you can decide to free yourself from the bonds of a love-hate relationship that has made you lose time and time again. The people mentioned in the first chapter all made their decisions. Some came slower than others, but the decisions were made and acted upon. Here is what happened when those caught in the love-hate trap decided to stop the massacre of their own identities.

SARAH: BUCKS, BOOZE, AND A BROKEN HEART

Sarah finally confronted her father about his drinking. She explained her hurt over being bought off when she needed time and attention. She told her dad of her worth and of her needs. She related to him her desires for his drinking to stop. She showed him what their relationship could be like and convinced him it was not too late to begin. Sarah's father obtained treatment because of her decision to do the best she could with the situation. It not only began their relationship; it saved her father's life.

MARY: ABANDONED IN RAGE

Mary resolved her rage through the help of her pastor. He helped her imagine the situation of her father and what stresses might have existed that led him to abandon her. She was able to accept that her father's mistake did not make her perfect and that she was capable of the same type of behaviors. This decision to resolve her rage with her father freed her to develop a wonderful relationship with her stepfather, a man who grew to love her deeply and accept her completely.

JOE AND BETTY: PERPLEXED PARENTS

Joe and Betty finally gave up on trying to change their son, Daren. Rather than focus on the problems, they began to shower him with acceptance. Behaviors that were wrong were punished. But no emphasis was placed on his appearance. Then they decided to focus time and attention on themselves. Rather than allowing Daren to drain their energy and hurt their own relationship, they decided to develop their love and mature their relationship. The ripeness was incredible. Daren responded, probably more to their stressing the importance of their own relationship than to anything else. He drove out the hate from the love-hate that once plagued the family. It finally became a family where peace, not war, remained.

DAN: TROUBLED EMPLOYEE

Dan was held captive by his boss, who had moved him up the ranks but would always insist he remain one rank below him. Dan's self-confidence was slowly being eroded until he finally made the decision to leave. And leave he did, but only after he had secured a better position in another company. His boss could not believe it and tried to dissuade him with new promises, but Dan stuck to his new course and thrived in his new job. Ironically, his old boss was out of work within one year of Dan's departure. Because of Dan's decision, Dan was able to earn all the compensation that had previously been shared between him and his old boss. He no longer made a living for anyone but himself.

SANDRA: SLEEPING WITH THE PAST

Sandra wised up and finally saw the faulty thinking and insecurity that held her to her husband even though he had abandoned her. When her divorce was finalized, she began working on the issues that had troubled her, and soon after she met a new man for her and her boys. They married and grew as her first husband sank deeper into his own problems. He was never heard from again. The boys were adopted by her new husband. Her decision to free herself from the past was the beginning of safety and security and love for herself and her boys.

MARILYN: OH GOD!

Marilyn made the decision to move on. She moved beyond her hurt and embarrassment over an adulterous husband. She was able to see that the situation was not God's desire but a result of the way things ironically happen in an imperfect world. She accepted God as a Father who would help her through any crisis but would not make her immune to them. Slowly she was restored to a caring, energetic person who set out to start over. She moved from the town that had victimized her with its gossip. She did not question God over her husband's death again. In her new town she became quite active in the church. She found peace after she had made the decision to look for it.

CARRYING THE MESSAGE

Once you join the crowd of people who work through and resolve their love-hate relationships, you have a need to share your experience with others in order to motivate them and encourage them. Life is never the same when you the take the focus off your hurts and put it on helping others. You create a new mission in life for yourself: a mission of helping others see what you have come to know, that anyone can decide to change. Life can be better. Relationships can be healed. And when you carry the message, you will have the intense satisfaction of watching others grow. Your pain then becomes the birth of a new relationship for you and those you help. But if you want to experience the joy, you have a decision to make.

About the Authors

STEPHEN F. ARTERBURN, MEd, is the founder and chairman of New Life Treatment Centers, Inc. The company offers Christ-centered care for adults and adolescents dealing with depression, abuse, eating disorders, compulsive sexual behavior, and drug and alcohol addiction. He is the author and co-author of ten books, including *Hooked on Life, Drug-Proof Your Kids, Toxic Faith, Addicted to Love,* and *The Angry Man.* Stephen serves on the board of directors for Overcomers Outreach, Naaman's Fellowship, and the National Council on Sexual Addiction, and he is on the advisory board for the National Association for Christian Recovery. Mr. Arterburn received his bachelor's degree from Baylor University and his master's degree from the University of North Texas, and he studied Christian counseling at Southwestern Theological Seminary. He lives in Laguna Beach, California, with his wife, Sandy, and their daughter, Madeline.

DAVID A. STOOP, Phd, is a clinical psychologist in private practice in Newport Beach, California. Dr. Stoop is director of Minirth-Meier-Stoop Clinic and a program director of the Minirth-Meier Clinic West. He holds degrees from Stetson University, Fuller Theological Seminary, and the University of Southern California. His publications include *Hope for the Perfectionist, Self-Talk: Key to Personal Growth,* and *The*

Angry Man. He and his wife, Jan, have led seminars on personal growth and relationships across the United States and in Australia and France. They are the parents of three sons and grandparents of two.